MCQs On Forensic Medicine and Toxicology

ARCHANA SINGH

Copyright © 2020 Archana Singh

All rights reserved.

ISBN: 9798678479709

MCQs on Forensic Medicine and Toxicology

First Edition: 2020

© Publisher

Whole book or any part of this book may not be reproduced or modified or transmitted in any form, such as recording, photocopying or copying by any other platform of any type of system whether it is electronic or in offline medium without permission of author of this book.

Price: 1000/-
US $: $13.33

Disclaimer

The author and editor have tried best to provide every information which is true to their knowledge related to the subject. Although author and editor ensure the optimum accuracy of the information and made every effort to retain the right information, yet it may be possible that some errors might have left.

The publisher, the printer, the author and the editor will not be held responsible for any error or inaccuracies.

MCQs on Forensic Medicine and Toxicology

Description

The "MCQs on Forensic Medicine and Toxicology" provides access to the questions which have been asked and can be asked in upcoming examinations, such as, NET/JRF, FACT, or other exams in which these subjects are in demand. It consist 1000 MCQs on Forensic Medicine And Forensic Toxicology.

This book is divided into two parts. Part I consists of 500 MCQs of relevant to the Forensic Medicine and Part II consists of 500 MCQs of relevant to the Forensic Toxicology. This book will help you to qualify NET/JRF examination as well as other competitive examination related to Forensic Medicine and Forensic Toxicology.

Edited By *@forensicfield*

Contact us:
Contactforensicscience@gmail.com
https://forensicfield.blog/
https://forensicfield.blogspot.com/
https://www.youtube.com/c/ForensicField/
https://www.facebook.com/forensicfield/
https://twitter.com/ForensicField
https://www.instagram.com/forensicfield/
https://www.linkedin.com/in/forensicfield/
https://forensicfield.tumblr.com/

MCQs on Forensic Medicine and Toxicology

Chapter

1 Forensic Medicine   1-109

2 Forensic Toxicology   110-201

Reference

MCQs on Forensic Medicine and Toxicology

Part 1

Forensic Medicine

1. Forensic Medicine is also known as:

    a.) Medical Jurisprudence

    b.) law of medicine

    c.) Forensic biology

    d.) Medicine

2. Who is the Father of Legal Medicine?

    a.) Hippocrates

    b.) Manu

    c.) Paolo Zacchia

    d.) Francois-Emmanuelle Fodere

3. Who is the Father of Surgery?

    a.) Al-Zahrawi

    b.) Sushruta

    c.) Manu

    d.) Hippocrates

4. 'Hidden causes of Disease', A Book on Forensic Pathology is written by:

    a.) Michelangelo

    b.) Antonio Benivieni

    c.) Andrea Vesalius

    d.) Theophile Bonet

5. Forensic Pathology deals with:

    a.) Interpretation of autopsy findings in a medico legal investigations

    b.) It deals with Viscera analysis

    c.) It deals with body fluids examination

d.) It deals with medicine

6. Who is the father of occupational medicine?

    a.) Paracelsus

    b.) Mathieu Orfila

    c.) Bernardino Ramazzini

    d.) Oswald Schmiedeberg

7. Forensic Medicine deals with the :

    a.) All types of Medicine.

    b.) Application of medical knowledge for Legal Proceedings.

    c.) Postmortem Reports

    d.) For purpose of research

8. Forensic medicine is a:

    a.) Branch of forensic science

    b.) Application of forensic science

    c.) A tool

    d.) Medium of crime scene investigation

9. An examination of a dead body, by a doctor is called:

    a.) Postmortem examination

    b.) Autopsy examination

    c.) Antemortem examination

    d.) Inquest

    e.) a & b

10. Forensic Medicine was first practiced in ancient India by:

    a.) Aristotle

    b.) Manu

c.) Chankya

d.) Charak

11. Study of Death is known as:

    a.) Entomology

    b.) Forensic Medicine

    c.) Toxicology

    d.) Thantology

12. First Medicolegal Autopsy was done by

    a.) Bartolomeo da Varignana

    b.) Dr. Buckeley

    c.) Alfred Swaine Taylor

    d.) Johann Ludwig Casper

13. A painter who did some autopsy to learn anatomy of human is:

    a.) Pablo Picasso

    b.) Vincent van Gogh

    c.) Leonardo da Vinci

    d.) Claude Monet

14. The word Autopsy is derived from the Greek word "Autopsia". Which means:

    a.) Postmortem

    b.) Dissection Of Body

    c.) The act of seeing for oneself

    d.) Operation

15. The application of entomology was first reported by:

    a.) Louis Francois Etienne Bergeret

b.) William Spence

c.) William Kirby

d.) Charles Darwin

16. In most cases, forensic entomology will only determine a:

    a.) Approximate PMI

    b.) Maximum PMI

    c.) Minimum PMI

    d.) Probable PMI

17. Before 72 hours, Besides of following evidence, livor mortis, algor mortis and rigor mortis are used:

    a.) Anthropological

    b.) Pathological

    c.) Odontological

    d.) Entomological

18. Which type of autopsy is performed to solve mysterious and unnatural death?

    a.) Clinical Autopsy

    b.) Medico legal Autopsy

    c.) Anatomical Autopsy

    d.) Postmortem

19. Autopsy is done of:

    a.) Asked body parts

    b.) Contested body parts

    c.) Permitted body parts

    d.) Whole Body

Forensic Medicine

20. Autopsy is requested by the Police under section:

    a.) 174 of Indian evidence act

    b.) 174 of criminal procedure code

    c.) 174 of Indian Penal Code

    d.) 174 of Police Code

21. Autopsy is requested by the Magistrate under section:

    a.) 176 of Indian evidence act

    b.) 176 of criminal procedure code

    c.) 176 of Indian Penal Code

    d.) 176 of Police Code

22. The goal of forensic autopsies is:

    a.) For ritual

    b.) For identification

    c.) For legal purpose

    d.) To determine whether death is natural or not

23. Virtual Autopsy is known as:

    a.) Vitopsy

    b.) Video autopsy

    c.) Virtopsy

    d.) Viropsy

24. Following tools are used in Virtopsy, except:

    a.) 3D Surface Scanner

    b.) MRI

    c.) Gas Chromatography

    d.) CT Scans

Forensic Medicine

25. To conduct postmortem examination an authorization letter is necessary in India, from:

    a.) Magistrate

    b.) Police Officer

    c.) Chief Justice

    d.) Any of the above

26. Best Method of Identification is:

    a.) DNA Fingerprint

    b.) Fingerprint

    c.) Face Recognition

    d.) Old Wounds

27. The fingerprint pattern may be impaired permanently in case of:

    a.) Eczema

    b.) Scalds

    c.) Scabies

    d.) Leprosy

28. Which disorder causes no fingerprints since birth?

    a.) Adermatoglyphia

    b.) Psoriasis

    c.) Eczema

    d.) Scleroderma

29. Postmortem examination should be Performed in:

    a.) UV Light

    b.) IR Light

    c.) Day Light

Forensic Medicine

d.) Any of the above

30. Postmortem examination should not be Performed in artificial light if possible, because it might conceal:

    a.) Certain shades of color

    b.) Truth

    c.) Hidden information

    d.) Any of the above

31. Time between death and examination of body:

    a.) Postmortem Interval

    b.) Time since death

    c.) Autopsy

    d.) Antimortem Interval

32. Procedure of lawful disinterment or digging out of a buried body from the grave is known as:

    a.) Cremation

    b.) Exhumation

    c.) Postmortem

    d.) Autopsy

33. Which one of the following is not empowered to order for exhumation:

    a.) Subdivisional Magistrate

    b.) Tehsildar

    c.) District Magistrate

    d.) Police Officer

34. What is a time limit for exhumation in India?

    a.) 10 years

b.) 20 years

c.) 5 years

d.) No limit

35. Which of the following is not a constituent of embalming fluid?

    a.) Eosin

    b.) Glycerin

    c.) Wax

    d.) Formalin

36. After completion of Embalming procedure following can't be made out:

    a.) Analysis of Blood

    b.) Interpretation of injury/disease

    c.) a & b

    d.) None of the above is true

37. In Embalming Composition Eosin use as a:

    a.) Perfume

    b.) Vehicle

    c.) Dye

    d.) Anticoagulant

38. In Embalming Composition which one of the following is use as a Vehicle:

    a.) Water

    b.) Glycerin

    c.) Formalin

    d.) Sodium Borate

39. Minimum quantity of blood required to be preserved for chemical examination is:

    a.) 10 ml

    b.) 5 ml

    c.) 1 ml

    d.) 50 ml

40. At what temperature blood should be preserved?

    a.) 2^0c

    b.) 4^0c

    c.) 0^0c

    d.) 1^0c

41. After death following decreases in blood level:

    a.) Potassium

    b.) Magnesium

    c.) Sodium

    d.) Glucose

42. What is the number of true ribs in human body?

    a.) 12

    b.) 14

    c.) 15

    d.) 16

43. From vitreous humor, estimation of time since death is done by:

    a.) Potassium

    b.) Magnesium

    c.) Sodium

d.) Glucose

44. If Fluid begins leaked from openings as cell membrane rupture, skin slays off, Time Since Death is:

    a.) 1-2 days

    b.) 2-4 days

    c.) 6-10 days

    d.) 30 minutes – 1 hour

45. Potassium deficiency is known as:

    a.) Hyperglycemia

    b.) Hypocalcaemia

    c.) Uremia

    d.) Hypokalemia

46. What is professional death sentence:

    a.) Erasure of name from the professional register due to any offence

    b.) Death sentence passed by court

    c.) Death by professional killer

    d.) Death in profession

47. Immediate sign of death is:

    a.) Fall in body temperature

    b.) Cessation of circulation and respiration

    c.) Stop breathing

    d.) Dilation of pupil

48. In new born babies, during autopsy body cavity to be opened first:

    a.) Depend on case

    b.) Skull

c.) Abdominal cavity

d.) Bone marrow

49. Greenish discoloration in post mortem is due to:

    a.) Methemoglobin

    b.) Sulf-Methemoglobin

    c.) Aniline

    d.) Nitrites

50. Ventricular fibrillation is the most frequent cause of _____.

    a.) Sudden Cardiac Arrest

    b.) Paralysis

    c.) Brain Hemorrhage

    d.) Diarrhea

51. Which of the following test compares weight of the lungs to the body:

    a.) Hydrostatic Test

    b.) Stomach Bowel Test

    c.) Breslau's Second Life Test

    d.) Fodere's Test

52. This test is done to confirm whether the lungs have undergone respiration in newborn or not:

    a.) Hydrostatic Test

    b.) Stomach Bowel Test

    c.) Breslau's Second Life Test

    d.) Fodere's Test

53. Confirmatory sign of Live Birth is:

    a.) Closure of Foetal channels

b.) Macerated Skin

c.) Exfoliation of Skin

d.) a & c

54. Skeleton is divided into:

    a.) 2

    b.) 4

    c.) 1

    d.) 3

55. "Teeth are Bone", this statement is:

    a.) Right

    b.) Wrong

    c.) Neither right nor wrong

56. 80% bone of Human Skeleton makes of:

    a.) Compact Bone

    b.) Spongy Bone

    c.) Bone Marrow

    d.) All of the above

57. If a person is dead within 30 minute from start of fire, reason of death can be:

    a.) Asphyxia

    b.) Broncho-pneumonia

    c.) Burn

    d.) Neurogenic shock

58. In a charred body, which of the following is useful in its identification:

    a) Comparison of Postmortem X-Rays with dental records

    b) Skull Identification

c) Bone marrow

d) Skeletal Features

59. Dental formula for permanent teeth is:

    a.) 2102

    b.) 2321

    c.) 2123

    d.) 2121

60. Hardest substance in human body is:

    a.) Keratin

    b.) Chondrin

    c.) Osteon

    d.) Enamel

61. Skeletonization will never occur in:

    a.) Climate Temperature

    b.) Subzero Temperature

    c.) Tropical Temperature

    d.) Thermodynamic Temperature

62. PM identification is difficult in case of:

    a.) Severe burns

    b.) Multiple stab wounds

    c.) Complete charring

    d.) Complete Putrefaction

63. Dry burn is caused by:

    a.) Hot liquid or steam

    b.) Flame or hot metals

c.) Deep X-Ray or UV-Rays

d.) Strong acids or alkalies

64. Colliquative Liquefaction is seen within:

    a.) 1 minute

    b.) 1 hour

    c.) 1 week

    d.) 1 month

65. Expert witness defines in:

    a.) Sec 45 IEA, 1872

    b.) Sec 48 IEA, 1872

    c.) Sec 47 IEA, 1872

    d.) Sec 46 IEA, 1872

66. Following Section is related to Dowry Death:

    a.) 300 IPC

    b.) 302 IPC

    c.) 299 IPC

    d.) 304 B IPC

67. Person is legally dead if he is not found for:

    a.) 30 years

    b.) 15 years

    c.) 5 years

    d.) 7 years

68. McNaughton's rule given in following section of Indian Penal Code, 1860:

    a.) 84

    b.) 85

    c.) 86

d.) 87

69. Medical Certificate is a:

    a.) Legal Document

    b.) Documentary Evidence

    c.) Oral evidence

    d.) Doctor's Certificate

70. All are exempted from oral testimony, except;

    a.) Dying Declaration

    b.) Medical evidences of injury as witness

    c.) Chemical examination report

    d.) Evidence of medical expert in lower court

71. Corpus Delicti Means:

    a.) The body of Offence

    b.) Dead Corpse

    c.) Delicate Corpse

    d.) All of the Above

72. Heaviest and largest internal organ of human body is:

    a.) Brain

    b.) Liver

    c.) Kidney

    d.) Large intestine

73. Largest organ of the human body is:

    a.) Skin

    b.) Liver

    c.) Large intestine

d.) Kidney

74. Identical Twins may not have:

    a.) Identical DNA fingerprint

    b.) Identical Blood group

    c.) Identical Fingerprint

    d.) Identical Appearance

75. Mummification occurs when the climate is:

    a.) Hot & Dry

    b.) Cold & Dry

    c.) Moist

    d.) Hot

76. Odour of mummified body is:

    a.) Pungent

    b.) Putrid

    c.) Offensive

    d.) Odorless

77. Cerebrospinal Fluid (CSF) in autopsy may be removed by:

    a.) Lumbar puncture

    b.) Withdrawing Fluid from Cisterna Magna

    c.) Puncturing the lateral ventricles directly

    d.) All of the above are correct.

78. Radiological signs of fetal death includes all of the following, except:

    a.) Overlapping of skull bones

    b.) Gross distortion of fetal anatomy

    c.) Fever & Cold

d.) Thrombus in fetal heart

79. Specific Gravity of Human body is:

    a.) 1.05

    b.) 2.08

    c.) 1.08

    d.) 1.0

80. Closure of coronal suture starts at the age of:

    a.) 10-12 years

    b.) 15-25 years

    c.) 24-40 years

    d.) 40-50 years

81. All of the following are found in brain dead patients, except;

    a.) Decreased Deep Tendon Reflex

    b.) Absent Papillary Reflexes

    c.) Complete Apnea

    d.) Heart unresponsive to Atropine

82. Following is not a reliable option for estimation of age:

    a.) Sternum

    b.) Sutural Closure

    c.) Frontanelle

    d.) Skull Suture

83. Following elements are found in DNA, Except:

    a.) Oxygen

    b.) Carbon

    c.) Sulphur

d.) Phosphorus

84. Statement 1: Teeth are considered best for DNA analysis in Case of Mass disasters.

    Statement 2: The cellular material of pulp cavity may remain unaffected.

    a.) Both statement is Right
    b.) Both statement is Wrong
    c.) First part is right second part is wrong
    d.) First part is wrong second part is right

85. Union of epiphysis in Head of Humerus occurs at the age of:

    a.) 10 years
    b.) 17 years
    c.) 5 years
    d.) 25 years

86. Which one of the following elements is required by our body for normal functioning of some enzymes?

    a.) Mercury (Hg)
    b.) Zinc (Zn)
    c.) Lead (Pb)
    d.) Antimony (Sb)

87. Following enzyme is present in tears:

    a.) Trypsin
    b.) Lysozyme
    c.) Maltase
    d.) Lipases

88. pH of seminal fluid is

a.) 7.4

b.) 7.0

c.) 2.0

d.) 6.5

89. Weight of dry Skeleton in adult human males is:

   a.) 10-12kg

   b.) 12.5kg-15kg

   c.) 2.5kg-5kg

   d.) 1kg-3kg

90. Which of the following is a future of apoptosis?

   a.) Cellular Swelling

   b.) Karyolysis

   c.) Chromatin Condensation

   d.) Associated inflammatory changes

91. "Nutmeg Liver" refers to

   a.) Chronic Venous congestion

   b.) Jaundice

   c.) Septicemia

   d.) Pneumonia

92. Fatty change:

   a.) Does not impair cellular function

   b.) Is most commonly due to diabetes

   c.) Only occurs in lever

   d.) Is caused by alcohol by an increase in intracellular alpha glycerol phosphate.

Forensic Medicine

93. The animal eaten parts of the body may be mistaken for ante mortem injury, Which is known as:

    a.) Injury

    b.) Animal Bite

    c.) Pseudo abrasion

    d.) Animal abrasion

94. About abrasions following statements are correct, except;

    a.) Abrasion on victim may show the length of the fingernails of assailant.

    b.) Abrasions are sign of struggle

    c.) Abrasions only made by weapon

    d.) Gunshot wound also made abrasion

95. Blood usually remains fluid after death, except:

    a.) Chronic Venous congestion

    b.) Jaundice

    c.) Septicemia

    d.) Pneumonia

96. Last structure to be autopsied in asphyxial death:

    a.) Head

    b.) Throax

    c.) Abdomen

    d.) Neck

97. The Last Sense a dying person loses is:

    a.) Sight

    b.) Smell

    c.) Hearing

d.) Touch

98. The Second Last Sensation a dying person is loses is:

   a.) Sight

   b.) Smell

   c.) Hearing

   d.) Touch

99. Chicken Fat Clot is:

   a.) Blood clot in chicken

   b.) Fatty Acid

   c.) Postmortem Blood Clot

   d.) Chicken Meat

100. Bertillon system is employed basing on:

   a.) Measurement of Hand

   b.) Measurement of Leg

   c.) Measurement of Body Parts

   d.) Measurement of Face

101. Absorption Elution Technique is used for:

   a.) Detection of seminal stain

   b.) Detection of Blood Stain

   c.) Detection of vaginal stain

   d.) Detection of Faecal stain

102. The best bones for determining sex are:

   a.) Sternum & Humerus

   b.) Clavicle & Tibia

   c.) Femur & Ulna

d.) Skull & pelvis

103. Most useful body part for sex determination is:

    a.) Femur

    b.) Pelvis

    c.) Tibia fibula

    d.) Skull

104. Sex chromatin is found in:

    a.) Lymphocytes

    b.) Erythrocytes

    c.) Monocytes

    d.) Leucocytes

105. A body which feels warm & stiff has been dead:

    a.) 2-3 hours

    b.) 3-8 hours

    c.) After 1 hour

    d.) More than 24 hours

106. In Algor Mortis, Algor means:

    a.) Death

    b.) Dead Body

    c.) Coldness

    d.) Heat of Body

107. Algor Mortis appears in dead body:

    a.) When temperature of the body start to decrease

    b.) When temperature of the body start to increase

    c.) When temperature of the body constant

Forensic Medicine

    d.) When temperature of body is 0^0

108. Rigor Mortis appears First in:

    a.) Abdominal wall

    b.) Hands

    c.) Eyelids

    d.) Legs

109. Rigor Mortis can be delayed by:

    a.) Obesity

    b.) Thinness

    c.) Race

    d.) Stature

110. Putrefaction is of:

    a.) 1 types

    b.) 2 types

    c.) 3 types

    d.) 4 types

111. Black Putrefaction occurs in dead body after:

    a.) 4-10 days

    b.) 10-20 days

    c.) 20-30 days

    d.) 30-40 days

112. In Rigor Mortis, Rigor means:

    a.) Death

    b.) Dead body

    c.) Coldness

d.) Rigidity

113. Rigor Mortis Completes in:

    a.) 2 hours

    b.) 6 hours

    c.) 8 hours

    d.) 12 hours

114. Immediate rigidity in a group of muscles without passing into stage of primary relaxation is:

    a.) Cadaveric Rigidity

    b.) Cadaveric Spasm

    c.) Rigor Mortis

    d.) Mummification

115. Cadaveric Spasm:

    a.) Develop immediately after death

    b.) Involves individual group of muscles

    c.) May develop hours after death

    d.) a & b

116. Which one of the following chemical found in the muscles is used and not reproduce after death, is reason of rigor mortis:

    a.) Calcium

    b.) Glycogen

    c.) Potassium

    d.) Magnesium

117. Rigor Mortis Appears in dead body:

    a.) Within 1-2 hours

b.) Within 2-6 hours

c.) Within 15-30 Minutes

d.) Anytime

118. Arrange in the proper order Rigor Mortis Spreads in the dead body in the following order:

   i. Lower Limbs

   ii. Chest

   iii. Eyelids

   iv. Lower Jaw

   Code:

   a.) (i), (ii), (iii) & (iv)

   b.) (iii), (iv), (ii) & (i)

   c.) (iv), (ii), (iii) & (i)

   d.) (ii), (i), (iv) & (iii)

119. Rigor Mortis is not seen in:

   a.) Old Person (above 70 years)

   b.) Child

   c.) Pregnant women

   d.) Fetus (less than 7 months)

120. A dead born fetus (less than 7 month) does not have:

   a.) Rigor Mortis

   b.) Mummification

   c.) Maceration

   d.) Adipocere Formation

121. Adipocere may be seen in:

a.) Body exposed to open

b.) Body buried in damp, clay soil

c.) Burial in dry hot air

d.) Prolonged immersion water

122. It develops 15 minutes after death and is the Ist Postmortem sign of death in Caucasian Person.

a.) Livor Mortis

b.) Algor Mortis

c.) Pallor Mortis

d.) Rigor Mortis

123. How many days does it take the eyeball to turn to liquid?

a.) 2 days

b.) 3 days

c.) 6-10 days

d.) 1 week

124. Pallor Mortis occurs in:

a.) Person with dark skin

b.) Person with Tan Skin

c.) Person with Normal Skin

d.) Person With Light/White Skin

125. In "Pallor Mortis", "Pallor" Means:

a.) Rigidness

b.) Paleness

c.) Stoppage of Pulse

d.) Brown Bluish Discolouration

Forensic Medicine

126. Livor Mortis appears in dead body:

    a.) Within 20-30 minutes

    b.) Within 1-2 hours

    c.) Within 2-6 hours

    d.) Anytime

127. Reddish-bluish staining of low lying dependent regions of the body, known as:

    a.) Rigor Mortis

    b.) Livor Mortis

    c.) Algor Mortis

    d.) Pallor Mortis

128. How long after death does lividity become permanent?

    a.) 30 minutes

    b.) 1 hours

    c.) 2 hours

    d.) 8 hours

129. Luminol reacts with hydrogen salt and forms in _____ Luminol Test:

    a.) Anion

    b.) Cation

    c.) Di-anion

    d.) Ion

130. The cooling of body is best represented by following curve when temperature and time does not match:

    a.) Sigmoid Curve

    b.) Circular

c.) Linear

d.) Any of the Above

131. The temperature of the dead body is measured using:

   a.) Medical Thermometer

   b.) Thanatometer

   c.) Pacifier Thermometer

   d.) Infrared Thermometer

132. The Temperature ideally preferred to preserve the body for autopsy is:

   a.) 4^0c

   b.) 0^0c

   c.) -4^0c

   d.) 1^0c

133. Chronological order of Postmortem changes after death is:

   a. Loss of reflexes, foul smell, adipocere and hypostasis

   b. Loss of reflexes, hypostasis, foul smell, and adipocere

   c. Foul smell, hypostasis, Loss of reflexes and adipocere

   d. Adipocere, Loss of reflexes, foul smell and hypostasis

134. Hypostasis is last for _____:

   a.) Few Hours

   b.) Days

   c.) Week

   d.) Months

135. _____ is used as medicine in Mental illnesses like Schizophrenia, Bipolar disorder and Depression:

   a.) Benzene

b.) Lithium

c.) Arsenic

d.) Barium

136. Gene Mutations caused by chemicals initiates the process of carcinogenesis. Which kinds of genes are mutated in this process?

   a.) Oncogenes

   b.) Protooncogenes

   c.) Tumor suppressor genes

   d.) b & c

137. Rule of Hasse is used to determine:

   a.) Age of fetus

   b.) The age of adult

   c.) For identification

   d.) Height of person

138. Time since death is calculated by multiplying drop in rectal temperature with:

   a.) 0.67

   b.) 2

   c.) 0.37

   d.) 0.46

139. Rectal temperature does not fall till what time after death?

   a.) 15-30 minutes

   b.) 30-60 minutes

   c.) 60-90 minutes

   d.) Immediately after death

Forensic Medicine

140. The rate of cooling of dead body in normal weather is:
    a.) 1.5°F/hour
    b.) 4.5°F/hour
    c.) 2.5°F/hour
    d.) 0.5°F/hour

141. The following situations are associated with rise of temperature after death:
    a.) Heat Stroke
    b.) Strychnine poisoning
    c.) Septicemia
    d.) All of the above

142. Most accurate place to take the body temperature of the deceased:
    a.) Liver
    b.) Kidney
    c.) Intestine
    d.) Brain

143. Rate of cooling helps in determining:
    a.) Place of death
    b.) Time of death
    c.) Cause of death
    d.) Manner of death

144. Time when the cooling of the body is completed may vary according to:
    a.) The medium in which it is kept after death
    b.) Condition of the body itself

c.) Manner of death

d.) All of the above

145. Following bodies retains heat longer than usual:

   a.) Fat Bodies

   b.) Die from Lightning

   c.) a & b

   d.) Time is same for all types of dead bodies

146. Rigor mortis starts when muscle ATP is reduced below:

   a.) 15%

   b.) 5%

   c.) 50%

   d.) 100%

147. _____ is the main source of energy for muscle contraction:

   a.) ATP (Adenosine Triposhphate)

   b.) Food

   c.) Water

   d.) Vitamin's

148. After death, generation of ATP stops, but consumption of it :

   a.) also stops

   b.) Continues

   c.) Depends on body

   d.) Constant

149. Depressed fracture of skull results from blows with:

   a.) Heavy object with small striking surface

   b.) Heavy object with large striking surface

   c.) Small object with heavy striking surface

d.) Large object with light striking surface

150. Greenstick fracture is:

    a.) Wrist fracture

    b.) Fatigue fracture

    c.) Part of cortex is intact and other part is crumpled

    d.) Spiral fracture of long bone

151. Boxer's Fracture is:

    a.) Fracture of first metacarpal base

    b.) Fracture of fifth metacarpal neck

    c.) Fracture of third metacarpal neck

    d.) Fracture of first metacarpal neck

152. Hyoid fracture is common in

    a.) Choking

    b.) Hanging

    c.) Strangulation

    d.) b & c

153. All are reason for death due to suffocation, except:

    a.) Smothering

    b.) Throttling

    c.) Choking

    d.) Gagging

154. Fracture in hyoid bone and larynx indicate:

    a.) Suicidal Throttling

    b.) Accidental Throttling

    c.) Homicidal Throttling

d.) Manual Strangulation

155. Lynching is

    a.) Practiced in North America

    b.) Hanging on Tree

    c.) Practiced by white people on Negros

    d.) All

156. Bleeding from the nostril, Mouth and ears is common in

    a.) Hanging

    b.) Strangulation by Ligature

    c.) Garroting

    d.) Choking

157. In _____, a loop of thin string is thrown around the neck of the victim from back.

    a.) Garroting

    b.) Burking

    c.) Bansdola

    d.) Strangulation

158. Spanish windlass is practiced in which form of strangulation:

    a.) Bansdola

    b.) Garroting

    c.) Throttling

    d.) Mugging

159. Maximum congestion is seen in:

    a.) Hanging

    b.) Choking

c.) Strangulation

d.) Drowning

160. _____ is a form of strangulation where the neck is compressed in between two bamboos or other sticks, one in front and one from the back.

   a.) Garroting

   b.) Burking

   c.) Bansdola

   d.) Strangulation

161. Bansdola is a form of:

   a.) Homicidal Suffocation

   b.) Homicidal Strangulation

   c.) Homicidal Choking

   d.) Homicidal Hanging

162. Appearance of simulating ligature mark on the neck due to the postmortem staining is:

   a.) Garroting

   b.) Burking

   c.) Bansdola

   d.) Pseudo Strangulation

163. Holding the neck of victim when bend his elbow is known as:

   a.) Mugging

   b.) Bansdola

   c.) Garrotting

   d.) Throttling

164. "Café coronary" is

a.) A type of death due to choking

b.) Death due to drowning

c.) Sudden death

d.) Death due to Poisoning

165. A person suddenly starts coughing and choking while eating his food and died shortly after. Reason of death is:

a.) Choking

b.) Gagging

c.) Smothering

d.) Trauma

166. Impotence quad hoc means?

a.) Medically impotent

b.) Legally impotent

c.) Impotent toward a particular woman

d.) All of the above

167. Best indicator of antimortem drowning is:

a.) Froth In Nostrils

b.) Water in Lungs

c.) Hemolysis

d.) Water in stomach

168. Death occurs faster in:

a.) Salt Water Drowning

b.) Fresh Water Drowning

c.) Sea Water Drowning

d.) Warm Water Drowning

Forensic Medicine

169. Gettler's Test is used to diagnose death due to:

    a.) Hanging

    b.) Strangulation

    c.) Burns

    d.) Drowning

170. Which of the following is not true about fresh water drowning?

    a.) Hyperkalemia

    b.) Hypovolemia

    c.) Ventricular fibrillation

    d.) Hemolysis

171. Which of the following is not seen in salt water drowning?

    a.) Hyperkalemia

    b.) Progressive Hypovolemia

    c.) Circulatory collapse

    d.) Acute Pulmonary Edema

172. Washer man's hand and feet are commonly seen in case of drowning in

    a.) 2 – 3 hrs.

    b.) 24 – 48 hrs.

    c.) 18 – 24 hrs.

    d.) 6 – 12 hrs.

173. Autopsy findings of Drowning in sea water is:

    a.) Salty water in stomach

    b.) High Potassium in left Heart

    c.) High calcium in heart

    d.) All of the Above

Forensic Medicine

174. In drowning, the epidermis of the hands and feet is separated in the form of gloves and stocking after:

    a.) 2 min

    b.) 2 hrs.

    c.) 2 weeks

    d.) 2 months

175. What is dry drowning?

    a.) Death occurs in few days of submersion episode

    b.) Death occurs due to sudden immersion in cold water

    c.) Water does not enter in lungs because of laryngeal spasm

    d.) Seen in alcoholics due to drowning in shallow pool

176. Cutis anserine seen in :

    a.) Strangulation

    b.) Garroting

    c.) Drowning

    d.) Throttling

177. Gall bladder will be _____ in starvation in postmortem.

    a.) Distended

    b.) Normal

    c.) Stretched

    d.) Thick Walled

178. A young lady was found dead. Her body was cold & complete stiff. The expected time pass since death is:

    a.) 2-4 hrs.

    b.) 4-6 hrs.

    c.) 6-10 hrs.

d.) More than 10 hrs.

179. Viscera should be kept/Preserved in :

    a.) Glass bottle

    b.) Plastic container

    c.) Paper bag

    d.) Steel Can

180. Which disorder/disease is rare in women compared to the men:

    a.) Osteoporosis

    b.) Nyctalopia

    c.) Down Syndrome

    d.) Color Blindness

181. Permanent Infirmity means:

    a.) A dangerous stab wound

    b.) Loss of Organ Function

    c.) Loss of an Organ

    d.) b & c

182. The positive finding of burial of a living person is:

    a.) Marked pulmonary oedema

    b.) Rigidity of Body

    c.) Earth or sand in trachea and bronchi

    d.) Congestion of liver and spleen

183. Gordon's Classification deals with-

    a.) Stature

    b.) Fingerprints

    c.) Death

Forensic Medicine

   d.) Footprint

184. In wild life Forensics, identification of animals done by

   a.) Body Features

   b.) Pug Marks

   c.) Color

   d.) Twigs

185. Illegal way of trafficking animals

   a.) Poaching

   b.) Trafficking

   c.) Kidnapping

   d.) Smuggling

186. Psychological autopsy is?

   a.) Autopsy of brain and spinal cord

   b.) To inquire about the psychiatric illness of the deceased

   c.) Assessment to the mental state of deceased person before death

   d.) All of the above

187. Coup-Contrecoup Injury is:

   a.) Damage to the brain on both sides

   b.) Accidental injury on leg

   c.) Dislocation of bones

   d.) Paralysis

188. Duret Hemorrhages are found in:

   a.) Liver

   b.) Brain

   c.) Kidney

d.) Heart

189. Brain Bleed is known as:

   a.) Intracranial Hemorrhage

   b.) Subarachnoid Hemorrhage

   c.) Epidural Hematoma

   d.) Subdural Hematoma

190. Most common type of Intracranial hemorrhage:

   a.) Epidural Hemorrhage

   b.) Subarachnoid Hemorrhage

   c.) Epidural Hematoma

   d.) Subdural Hematoma

191. Statement 1- Hemorrhage: Copious discharge of blood from the blood vessels.

   Statement 2- Hematoma: Localized collection of blood in the tissues, usually to clotted or partially clotted.

   a.) Statement 1 is right while Statement 2 is wrong

   b.) Statement 1 is right while Statement 2 is wrong

   c.) Both Statements is Right

   d.) Both Statements is Wrong

192. Following tests are associated with cessation of circulation, except:

   a.) Magnus Test

   b.) I-Card's Test

   c.) Takayama Test

   d.) Diaphanous Test

193. Magnus test also known as:

a.) Fingernail Test

b.) I-Card's Test

c.) Ligature Test

d.) Transillumination Test

194. Transillumiation Test is also known as:

a.) Fingernail Test

b.) Diaphanous Test

c.) I Card's Test

d.) Ligature Test

195. Which test is associated with cessation of Breathing?

a.) Feather Test

b.) Mirror Test

c.) Winslow's Test

d.) All of the Above

196. Wreden's test is to demonstrate-

a.) Live birth

b.) Insanity

c.) Putrefaction

d.) Assault

197. Breslau's second life test utilizes:

a.) Liver

b.) Stomach

c.) Ear

d.) Lungs

198. For examination of diatoms sample should collect from:

- a.) Nasal Cavity
- b.) Epithelial Cells
- c.) Bone Marrow
- d.) Blood

199. Best body part for taking sample for diatom test:
    - a.) Lungs
    - b.) Stomach
    - c.) From any part of body
    - d.) Bone Marrow in Femur

200. Diatoms are:
    - a.) Algae
    - b.) Parasites
    - c.) Bacteria
    - d.) Fungi

201. Dirt Collar is seen in:
    - a.) Drowning
    - b.) Firearm Entry wound
    - c.) Mob Lynching
    - d.) All

202. Wounds on the left hand are suggestive of:
    - a.) Fabricated wound
    - b.) Defense wound
    - c.) Self-inflicted wound
    - d.) None

203. Postmortem Rigidity first starts in:

- a.) Upper Eyelids
- b.) Fingers
- c.) Hands
- d.) Mouth

204. Fracture-a-la-signature (or signature fracture) is a _____:
    - a.) Depressed Skull Fracture
    - b.) Finger Fracture
    - c.) Parkinson's
    - d.) None of the above

205. Gutter fracture can be seen in:
    - a.) Accident case
    - b.) Bullet injury
    - c.) Crushed skull
    - d.) Sharp weapon injury

206. Pond Fracture is also known as:
    - a.) Gutter fracture
    - b.) Hinge fracture
    - c.) Ping-Pong Ball Fracture
    - d.) None of the above

207. Pond fracture is seen in:
    - a.) Neonates and young children
    - b.) Adults
    - c.) Both
    - d.) None of the above

208. Statement 1: Children have 20 teeth, called temporary or milk teeth.

Statement 2: They are strong, broad and heavy.

a.) Both Statements are wrong

b.) Both Statements are Right

c.) Statement 1 is wrong but Statement 2 is right

d.) Statement 1 is Right but Statement 2 is wrong

209. Adipocere is Hydrogenation or saponification of fats, which occurs in:

a.) Bodies immersed in water

b.) Body buried in Soil

c.) Burnt body

d.) Body exposed in air

210. Which is true about Adipocere:

a.) Also called saponification

b.) Sweetish smell

c.) Occurs due to gradual hydrolysis and hydrogenation of fats

d.) All of the above

211. Adipocere formation is an _____:

a.) Biochemical Change

b.) Bacterial Process

c.) Enzymatic Process

d.) Accidental Phenomenon

212. The following term is used when Fetus die in the womb and its skin becomes soggy, wet, soft to touch:

a.) Adipocere

b.) Putrefaction

c.) Saponification

d.) Maceration

213. Spalding sign seen in:

    a.) Poisoning

    b.) Drowning

    c.) Maceration

    d.) Adipocere

214. Putrefaction is:

    a.) Autolysis of the body

    b.) Cooling of the body

    c.) Stiffening of the body

    d.) Foul smelling of the body

215. Putrefaction is facilitated by all, Except;

    a.) Very high temperature

    b.) Fresh air

    c.) Moist environment

    d.) Grave

216. Which solutions should be inject for the preservation of dead body and delaying the process of putrefaction for some time:

    a.) Formaldehyde

    b.) Anesthesia

    c.) Ceftriaxone Injection

    d.) Fluconazole

217. Color changes of Putrefaction are first observed in the:

    a.) Right iliac fossa

    b.) Popliteal fossa

c.) Cubital fossa

d.) Armpits

218. A process after death in which a corpse preserved through desiccation is known as:

a.) Skeletalisation

b.) Mummification

c.) Putrefaction

d.) Embalming

219. Place of destroyed tattoo mark can be inferred from the presence of pigment in:

a.) Outer layer of skin

b.) Epidermis

c.) Lymph nodes Regional

d.) Endodermis

220. Main cause of death in severe burn cases is:

a.) Fever

b.) Bacterial infection

c.) Dehydration

d.) b & c

221. Which one of the following will be a third degree burn?

a.) Burns extends through all the skin layers and tissue

b.) 90% of the body is burnt

c.) 5% are of body is burnt

d.) Joints of body are burnt

222. Which of the followings affect the seriousness of electric burn?

Forensic Medicine

a.) Type of electric current

b.) Exposed body surface area

c.) Age of the victim

d.) All of the above

223. Which finding in the body is suggestive of antemortem burns?

    a.) 100% burns

    b.) Soot in airways

    c.) Flexion of joints

    d.) None of the above

224. Casper's Dictum is used for

    a.) Estimation of Time since death

    b.) Cause of death

    c.) Identification of body

    d.) All of the above

225. Bones begin to decompose after death in :

    a.) After 3 years

    b.) After 6 Months

    c.) After 1 week

    d.) After 1 years

226. The speed of decomposition depend upon:

    a.) Body

    b.) Age

    c.) Nature of death

    d.) Environment

    e.) All Of The Above

227. The mechanism of death from cold is:

a.) Carboxy hemoglobin formation

b.) Respiratory Enzyme inhabitation

c.) CNS failure

d.) Paralysis

228. First internal organ to Putrefy is

a.) Liver

b.) Kidney

c.) Brain

d.) Larynx/Trachea

229. First sign of putrefaction is found:

a.) Below the liver

b.) Heart

c.) Spleen

d.) Kidney

230. Order of Putrefaction in Human body is:

a.) Heart-Brain-Uterus-Spleen

b.) Spleen-Brain-Heart-Uterus

c.) Heart-Spleen-Brain-Uterus

d.) Uterus-Heart-Spleen-Brain

231. Last Organ to Putrefy

a.) Testes

b.) Uterus/Prostate

c.) Ovary

d.) Kidney

232. Putrefaction occurs over the ceacal area after around:

- a.) 12 hours
- b.) 12-24 hours
- c.) 24-28 hours
- d.) 3 days

233. Chadwick's Sign is:
    - a.) Red bruise on Vagina
    - b.) Blue Coloration of Vagina
    - c.) Bruises on Body
    - d.) Stiffing of Body

234. Which locus is used for determining both male and female gender in DNA fingerprinting?
    - a.) DYS 19
    - b.) DYS-STR 393
    - c.) Y-plex Ladder
    - d.) Amelogenin

235. Joule Burns are seen in
    - a.) Electrocution
    - b.) Burn by flame
    - c.) Lightining
    - d.) 3rd degree burn

236. Suspended animation (when subject is alive but shows no sign of life) may be seen in:
    - a.) Hanging
    - b.) Strangulation
    - c.) Electrocution

d.) Murder

237. Confirmatory Sign of being burned alive is:

    a.) Smell of flammable substance from body

    b.) Burnt Clothes

    c.) Carbon particles in terminal bronchioles

    d.) Burnt skin

238. The characteristic difference between antemortem and postmortem clot is:

    a.) Color

    b.) Elasticity

    c.) Texture

    d.) Adhesion to vessel wall

239. Difference between antemortem and postmortem wound is:

    a.) Presence Of Chloride In Blister

    b.) Presence Of Cynhaemoglobin

    c.) Extravasation

    d.) Stain Removal Mechanically

240. Kevorkian sign is seen in?

    a.) Heart

    b.) Pupil

    c.) Retinal Vessels

    d.) Cornea

241. Kevorkian sign is seen by using an?

    a.) Microscope

    b.) Ophthalmoscope

Forensic Medicine

    c.) Magnifying Glass

    d.) All

242. Kevorkian sign is a _____.

    a.) Postmortem change

    b.) Antemortem change

    c.) Perimortem change

    d.) All of the above

243. Kevorkian sign appears in dead body_____.

    a.) It appears within hour after death and lasts for about 24 hour.

    b.) It appears within minutes after death and lasts for about 1 hour.

    c.) It appears within hour after death and lasts for about 7 hour.

    d.) It appears within seconds after death and lasts for about 4 hour.

244. Whiplash injury is caused due to:

    a.) Injury on Head

    b.) Acute hypertension of Spine

    c.) a & c

    d.) Hand injury

245. Hegar's sign is for the detection of

    a.) Early sign of Pregnancy

    b.) Dead Foetus

    c.) Complication of Pregnancy

    d.) Virginity

246. Failure of function of Brain in case of :

    a.) Asphyxia

    b.) Coma

c.) Syncope

d.) All of the above

247. Failure of function of Heart in case of :

a.) Asphyxia

b.) Coma

c.) Syncope

d.) All of the above

248. Failure of respiratory System in case of :

a.) Asphyxia

b.) Coma

c.) Syncope

d.) All of the above

249. All may cause traumatic asphyxia, except:

a.) Railway Accident

b.) Accidental Strangulation

c.) Road Accident

d.) All of the above

250. _____ is a general term referring to inadequate supply of Oxygen to the tissues or an impairment of the cellular utilization of oxygen for any reason.

a.) Hypoxemia

b.) Hypoxia

c.) Anoxia

d.) None

251. Marbling is due to:

a.) Clotting of blood in veins

b.) Lightening

c.) Veins becoming visible due to decomposition of blood

d.) All of the above

252. Types of hypoxia include:

   a.) Hypoxic hypoxia

   b.) Anemic hypoxic

   c.) Cytotoxic/Histotoxic hypoxia

   d.) Stagnant hypoxia

   e.) All Of the Above

253. In general, what type of drugs are psychotropic medications?

   a.) Acidic Drugs

   b.) Basic Drugs

   c.) Neutral Drugs

   d.) Methylated Drugs

254. _____ refers only to decreased carriage of oxygen in the arterial blood.

   a.) Hypoxemia

   b.) Hypoxia

   c.) Anoxia

   d.) None

255. Refractive index of hair is determined by

   a.) Microscopic examination

   b.) Florence Test

   c.) Beckline Method

d.) All of the above

256. Hair _____ to grow after death.

   a.) Start

   b.) Cease

   c.) Continue

   d.) More

257. Features which distinguishes human hair from animal hair is:

   a.) Equal diameter of medulla and cortex

   b.) Medulla is 1/3 or less of the shaft diameter

   c.) Pigments

   d.) Medulla is half or more of the shaft diameter

258. Burking is a particular method of homicidal smothering and traumatic asphyxiation, which is named after:

   a.) Burke and Hare

   b.) Burk and king

   c.) Burke and hang

   d.) Burke and Burke

259. Burking is derived from:

   a.) Place

   b.) Style use for murder

   c.) Weapon used for murder

   d.) Person

260. The postmortem finding seen in smothering:

   a.) Fracture of the body of hyoid

   b.) Abrasion on the inner side of the mouth

c.) Thyroid fracture

d.) Curved mark on the neck

261. Sexual asphyxia is associated with:

    a.) Sadism

    b.) Fetishism

    c.) Masochism

    d.) Voyeurism

262. Sexual asphyxia is:

    a.) Suicidal Death

    b.) Homicidal death

    c.) Natural death

    d.) Accidental death

263. The bleeding and tears from genitalia is indicative of:

    a.) Abortion

    b.) Instrumentation

    c.) Forced Sexual Intercourse

    d.) Self-inflicted injury

264. Bar Bodies are not seen in:

    a.) Down's Syndrome

    b.) Klinefelter Syndrome

    c.) Marfan's Syndrome

    d.) Turner Syndrome

265. Turner syndrome occurs in:

    a.) Male

    b.) Female

    c.) Both of the above

d.) None of the above

266. Tribadism is :

   a.) Female Homosexuality

   b.) Male Homosexuality

   c.) Homosexuality

   d.) None of the Above

267. Two Bar Bodies are seen in

   a.) XXX

   b.) XX

   c.) XO

   d.) XXY

268. Cephalic Index is useful for the determination of

   a.) Age

   b.) Race

   c.) Sex

   d.) Face

269. Race can be determined by the:

   a.) Complexion

   b.) Voice

   c.) Fingerprint

   d.) Footprint

270. Classical disorder of sex chromosome is:

   a.) Down's Syndrome

   b.) Klinefelter Syndrome

   c.) Marfan's Syndrome

d.) All of the above

271. Klinefelter Syndrome occurs in:

    a.) Male

    b.) Female

    c.) Both of the above

    d.) None of the above

272. Earliest bone to ossify is:

    a.) Femur

    b.) Clavicle

    c.) Tibia fibula

    d.) Pelvis

273. For bone age calculation in individuals aged 18-22 years, Radiographs are done of :

    a.) Clavicle

    b.) Elbow

    c.) Wrist

    d.) Knee

274. Pearson's Formula is Used for:

    a.) Age

    b.) Race

    c.) Sex

    d.) Stature

275. Which of the organ is commonly affected by shock waves?

    a.) Heart

    b.) Lungs

c.) Liver

d.) Brain

276. Which is not a Thermal Injury?

   a.) Heat stroke

   b.) Scalds

   c.) Contusion

   d.) Hypothermia

277. Which is not a Mechanical Injury?

   a.) Abrasion

   b.) Incised Wound

   c.) Firearm Wound

   d.) Burns

278. Lichtenberg Figures is an external lesion seen in?

   a.) Heat stroke

   b.) Radiation Injury

   c.) Lightning

   d.) Electrocution

279. Following markings are seen in Lichtenberg figures?

   a.) Burning marking

   b.) Blisters on skin

   c.) Burned and patchy skin

   d.) Superficial, thin, tortuous markings

280. Which type of pattern seen in Lichtenberg figures?

   a.) Circles

   b.) Sketchy lines

c.) Thorn like pattern

d.) Fern Leaf

281. Lichtenberg figures are also known as?

   a.) Lightning figures

   b.) Filigree burns

   c.) Radiography Burns

   d.) All of the above

282. Hanging is:

   a.) Suspension of body by ligature after death

   b.) Obliteration of air passage by external factor

   c.) Mechanical interference to respiration

   d.) Suspension of body by a ligature around the neck, body weight acting as constricting force

283. Ligature mark in hanging is:

   a.) Oval

   b.) Circular

   c.) Oblique

   d.) Straight

284. "Le Facie Sympathique" is seen in:

   a.) Hanging

   b.) Homicide

   c.) Dowry Death

   d.) Poisoning Case

285. A horizontal ligature mark is seen in the neck in case of hanging

   a.) In partial Hanging

b.) Throttling

c.) When a fixed loop with a single knot at the back of the head

d.) When a fixed loop with a single knot at the chin

286. In Judicial Hanging, fracture of vertebral column is usually seen between:

a.) C1 And C2

b.) C2 And C3

c.) C4 And C5

d.) C5 And C6

287. Simon sign is mainly seen in:

a.) Forcible Rape

b.) Oral Intercourse

c.) Infanticide

d.) Complete hanging

288. Coma occurs rapidly in hanging if ligature completely obstructs:

a.) Vertebral Arteries

b.) Jugular Veins

c.) Carotid Arteries

d.) None of the Above

289. When the body is suspended from a high point of suspension and feet are not touching ground, it is called:

a.) Complete Hanging

b.) Partial Hanging

c.) Typical Hanging

d.) Atypical Hanging

290. A male suspended himself. A ligature found around his neck and the knot was situated in region of occipital area this is known as:

   a.) Typical Hanging

   b.) Atypical Hanging

   c.) Strangulation

   d.) Asphyxia

291. In typical hanging knot is present at:

   a.) In front of ear

   b.) Mastoid area

   c.) Occipital Area

   d.) Thyroid cartilage

292. In case of typical hanging, post mortem hypostasis is seen in:

   a.) Hands and forearms

   b.) Legs and feet

   c.) Private parts

   d.) a & b

293. When the knot of the ligature is elsewhere, such as; right or left side of neck, it is known as:

   a.) Typical Hanging

   b.) Atypical Hanging

   c.) Complete Hanging

   d.) Partial Hanging

294. When some part of the body touches the ground, like; knees, feet, etc. It is known as:

   a.) Complete Hanging

b.) Partial Hanging

c.) Typical Hanging

d.) Atypical Hanging

295. Tardieu spots in hanging are not seen in:

a.) Scalp

b.) Eyebrow

c.) Chest wall

d.) Face

296. Tardieu spot disappear after:

a.) 1 hour

b.) 2 hour

c.) As rigor set in

d.) never

297. Increased salivation is seen in death due to:

a.) Strangulation

b.) Hanging

c.) Drowning

d.) Choking

298. A confirm sign of antemortem hanging is:

a.) Swollen and protrude tongue

b.) Protrude tongue and congested eyes

c.) A thin line of congestion of eyes hemorrhage along the edges of ligature mark

d.) Swollen hand and foot

Forensic Medicine

299. In Undertaker's Fracture, Tearing of vertebral column is usually seen between:
    a.) C1 And C2
    b.) C2 And C3
    c.) C4 And C5
    d.) C6 And C7

300. Undertaker's Fracture is basically a:
    a.) Antemortem Fracture
    b.) Postmortem Fracture
    c.) Perimortem Fracture
    d.) Fracture

301. Postmortem fracture differs from antemortem fracture by all, Except:
    a.) Absence Of Bleeding
    b.) Absence Of Granulation At Fracture Site
    c.) Laceration Over Skin
    d.) Absence Of Callus

302. Hangman's Fracture is mainly caused due to impacts of high force causing extension of the neck and great axial load onto the:
    a.) C1 And C2
    b.) C2
    c.) C3
    d.) C6 And C7

303. Teardrop sign is seen in:
    a.) Fracture media wall of orbit
    b.) Fracture lateral wall of orbit

- c.) Fracture floor of orbit
- d.) Fracture roof of orbit

304. Fracture in root of orbit is caused by:
    - a.) Blow on forehead
    - b.) Blow on Lower Jaw
    - c.) Fall on backside
    - d.) Blow on parietal region

305. Concussion causes:
    - a.) Small hemorrhages and swelling of brain tissues
    - b.) Momentary interruption of brain function with/without loss of consciousness
    - c.) Tearing or shearing of brain structures
    - d.) Bruising of the brain

306. Which one of the following is not a skull fracture type:
    - a.) Linear
    - b.) Depressed
    - c.) Basal
    - d.) Diffused axonal

307. Le Forte's Fracture would include all of the following, except;
    - a.) Maxilla
    - b.) Mandible
    - c.) Zygoma
    - d.) Nasal bones

308. Bumper fracture is:
    - a.) Primary Impact injury
    - b.) Secondary impact injury

c.) Tertiary impact injury

d.) Secondary injury

309. Motor Cyclist fracture also known as hinge fracture, occurs when:

   a.) Comminuted fracture of the vault

   b.) Skull base divided into 2 halves

   c.) Ring fracture

   d.) Gutter fracture

310. Sparrow foot marks are associated with which type of injury:

   a.) Motor cyclist fracture

   b.) Steering wheel impact

   c.) Wind screen impact

   d.) Under-running fracture

311. In Lacerated wound the hair bulb is:

   a.) Cut

   b.) Crushed

   c.) Dragged

   d.) Lacerated

312. Lanugo hair grows on:

   a.) Body of human fetus in womb

   b.) Body of an adult

   c.) Body of an animal

   d.) All of the above

313. Lanugo Hairs are:

   a.) Pigmented

   b.) Medullae

c.) Complex Scale Patterns

d.) Thin and Soft

314. In 'Crippen case', body of Cora Crippen was identified by:

a.) Tattoo mark

b.) Scar Tissue

c.) Color of eyes

d.) DNA Test

315. Which of the following is true regarding Superfecundation?

a.) The second fetus born later.

b.) Fertilization of ovum in an already pregnant woman

c.) Both ova do not always develop to maturity

d.) All of the above

316. Rigor mortis does not occur in fetus less than:

a.) 9 month

b.) 12 month

c.) 8 month

d.) 7 month

317. Putrefaction is brought about in a dead body by:

a.) Viruses

b.) Bacterial Action

c.) Moths

d.) Temperature

318. Chief agent for bacterial putrefaction is:

a.) E. coli

b.) B. fragilis

c.) C. Welchii

d.) Staph Aureus

319. Following organisms are responsible for putrefaction:

    a.) Staphylococcus

    b.) Streptococcus

    c.) C. Welchii

    d.) All of the Above

320. Putrefaction is slower in:

    a.) Water

    b.) Ground

    c.) Moist Place

    d.) None

321. Putrefaction is replaced Occasionally by:

    a.) Mummification

    b.) Rigor Mortis

    c.) Adipocere Formation

    d.) a & c

322. Putrefactive gases are all except:

    a.) CO_2

    b.) NO_2

    c.) H_2S

    d.) NH_3

323. The dead body start emitting unpleasant and foul smell due to formation and collection of following decomposition gas:

    a.) H_2S

    b.) Methane

c.) CO_2

d.) NH_3

e.) All of the Above

324. Decomposition in human body starts in:

   a.) Fresh Stage

   b.) Post-Decay Stage

   c.) Decay Stage

   d.) Bloat Stage

325. Postmortem hemolysis due to bacterial enzyme

   a.) Lecithinase

   b.) Phospholipase

   c.) Streptokinase

   d.) Hyaluronidase

326. Tsunami Lung is :

   a.) Death by explosion of lung, as if a tsunami is caused within the body

   b.) Severe systemic infections following aspiration pneumonia caused by near drowning in a Tsunami

   c.) Death due to drowning in Tsunami

   d.) Finding of both lungs separated completely from their bronchial attachments, seen most often in tsunamis.

327. _____ is fertilization of 2 ova discharged from the ovary at the same period by 2 separate acts of coitus committed at short intervals.

   a.) Superfertilization

   b.) Superfecundation

   c.) Superfetation

d.) Surrogacy

328. Contusion becomes yellow due to:

   a.) Bilirubin in the 5th day

   b.) Reduced hemoglobin in the 3rd day

   c.) Biliverdin in the 5th day

   d.) Bilirubin in the 1st day

329. _____ is the most reliable method for estimating blood alcohol level.

   a.) Cavett's Test

   b.) Breath Alcohol Anaylzer

   c.) Kozelka and Hine Test

   d.) Gas Liquid Chromatography

330. Tachie noire refers to:

   a.) Postmortem staining

   b.) Flaccidity of eyeball

   c.) Wrinkled dusty sclera

   d.) Maggot growth

331. Retraction balls after trauma are seen in:

   a.) Brain

   b.) Lung

   c.) Spleen

   d.) Liver

332. Apolexy is:

   a.) Learning disability

   b.) Insanity leading to commitment of a crime

c.) Sudden onset of bleeding in the brain

d.) Injury to the brain due to trauma

333. Brain hemorrhage limited by sutures

   a.) EDH (Epidural Hematoma)

   b.) SAH (Subarachnoid hemorrhage)

   c.) SDH (Subdural Hematoma)

   d.) ICH (Intracerebral Hemorrhage)

334. Petechial Hemorrhages may be seen in case of:

   a.) Peritoneum

   b.) Pericardium

   c.) Meninges

   d.) All of the above

335. Traumatic Bleeding may include all, except:

   a.) EDH (Epidural Hematoma)

   b.) SAH (Subarachnoid hemorrhage)

   c.) SDH (Subdural Hematoma)

   d.) ICH (Intracerebral Hemorrhage)

336. Vibices is also known as:

   a.) Poisoning

   b.) Postmortem Staining

   c.) Bruises

   d.) Tumor

337. Mineralization of teeth begins at:

   a.) Crown and progresses towards root

   b.) Root and progresses towards crown

c.) Simultaneously at root and crown

d.) Begins in the center

338. Rave drug is _____?

   a.) Poppy seeds

   b.) Ecstasy

   c.) Cannabis Sativa

   d.) Heroin

339. Which of the following is used for Narcoanalysis?

   a.) Scopolamine (Hyoscine)

   b.) Sodium thiopental (Sodium Pentothal)

   c.) Amobarbital (Amytal Sodium)

   d.) Secobarbital sodium (Seconal)

   e.) All of the above

340. Fertilization of a second ovum in a woman who is already pregnant is:

   a.) Superfertilization

   b.) Superfecundation

   c.) Superfetation

   d.) Surrogacy

341. Drug that is absolutely contradicted in pregnancy are:

   a.) Diazepam

   b.) Aspirin

   c.) Acetaminophen

   d.) Penicillin

342. Molecular Death refers to…

   a.) Death of Cells.

Forensic Medicine

- b.) Complete and irreversible cessation of the function of the brain, heart and the lungs.
- c.) Death of molecules.
- d.) Body stops working.

343. Somatic Death refers to…

- a.) Death of Cells.
- b.) Complete and irreversible cessation of the function of the brain, heart and the lungs.
- c.) Death of molecules.
- d.) Body stops working.

344. Apparent Death refers to…

- a.) Death of Cells.
- b.) Complete and irreversible cessation of the function of the brain, heart and the lungs.
- c.) Death of molecules.
- d.) That state in which breathing and functions of the heart are slowed down.

345. Somatic Death Also known as:

- a.) Molecular death
- b.) Clinical Death
- c.) Cellular Death
- d.) Sudden Death

346. Molecular Death Also known as:

- a.) Molecular death
- b.) Clinical Death

Forensic Medicine

    c.) Cellular Death

    d.) Sudden Death

347. Self-inflicted injury are known as:

    a.) Fabricated Injury

    b.) Forged Injury

    c.) Fictious Injury

    d.) All of the above

348. Blunt injury to abdomen:

    a.) Rarely Need Urgent Laparotomy

    b.) May Cause Intestinal Obstruction

    c.) May Cause Peritonitis

    d.) May Cause Gastroduodenal Ulceration

349. Death in blunt trauma chest is due to:

    a.) Tracheobronchial Injury

    b.) Pulmonary Contusions

    c.) Rupture Esophagus

    d.) Chylothorax

350. Which hormone is not released in Trauma:

    a.) Glucagon

    b.) GH

    c.) Thyroxin

    d.) ADH

351. Postmortem Luminescence is caused by:

    a.) Oleander

    b.) Armillaria

c.) Mercury

d.) Bacteria

352. Postmortem Luminescence is usually due to contamination of following bacteria:

   a.) Cl. Welchii

   b.) E. Coli

   c.) Photobacterium Fischeri

   d.) All of the above

353. Following Disease is caused by bacteria in Human Eye:

   a.) Glaucoma

   b.) Xerophthalmia

   c.) Trachoma

   d.) Protanopia

354. Hensen's cells are found in:

   a.) Liver

   b.) Spleen

   c.) Ear

   d.) Eye

355. Which one is not a clinical feature of raised intracranial features of raised intracranial tension?

   a.) Headache

   b.) Insomnia

   c.) Bradycardia

   d.) Papilloedema

Forensic Medicine

356. Headache that reaches its maximum intensity in less than 1 min and last about 5 minutes or more is:

    a.) Migraine Headaches

    b.) Post-Traumatic Headaches

    c.) Cluster Headaches

    d.) Thunderclap Headaches

357. In cold weather (below 2.5 to 0°c) when skin turns white and waxy or gray in color and mottled, but feels normal to touch. This condition known as:

    a.) Frostnip

    b.) Frostbite

    c.) Cold stroke

    d.) Cold bite

358. A condition in which skin and the tissue just below the skin freeze and hard to touch, is known as:

    a.) Frostnip

    b.) Frostbite

    c.) Cold stroke

    d.) Cold bite

359. Sledge Hammer Blow is seen in:

    a.) Poisoning

    b.) Lightning Flashes

    c.) Asphyxia

    d.) Firearm Injury

360. Cattle turking is seen in:

    a.) Coronary Blood Vessels

b.) Retinal Blood Vessels

c.) Eye

d.) Liver

361. Abortion stick causes abortion by the mechanism of:

    a.) Uterine contraction

    b.) Placental Abruption

    c.) Surgery

    d.) All of the above

362. Two parallel linear bruises separated by an undamaged skin. This is following type of Bruise:

    a.) Petechial Hemorrhages

    b.) Tramline Bruises

    c.) Intradermal Bruises

    d.) Pad Bruises

363. Distinct Marking of the tire on the body are defined as::

    a.) Petechial Hemorrhage

    b.) Patterned Abrasion

    c.) Pad Abrasion

    d.) Contusion

364. Foamy liver is characteristic of:

    a.) Adipocere

    b.) Saponification

    c.) Maceration

    d.) Putrefaction

365. More than 5% carboxy-hemoglobin is measured in an non-smoker adult; death is due to:

   a.) Arsenic Poisoning

   b.) Antemortem Burns

   c.) Methylene Chloride Poisoning

   d.) b & c

366. Swelling of the scalp in a newborn is known as:

   a.) Caput succedaneum

   b.) Cephalhematoma

   c.) Head Injury

   d.) Cone Head

367. Septal Defect is also known as:

   a.) Restricted blood flow

   b.) Hole in the Heart

   c.) Shortage of oxygen in body

   d.) Electrical impulses in the heart

368. Atherosclerosis is a:

   a.) Hardening and narrowing of arteries

   b.) Hole in heart

   c.) Restricted blood flow

   d.) Shortage of oxygen in body

369. A group of many heart disease that are present at birth is known as:

   a.) Atherosclerosis

   b.) Septal defect

   c.) Heart disease

d.) Cyanotic Heart Defect

370. Tachycardia is refers to:

    a.) Fast blood flow

    b.) Cardiac Arrest

    c.) Fast Heart Rate

    d.) Tache noire

371. Shearing damage is seen in:

    a.) Brain

    b.) Heart

    c.) Uterus

    d.) Gall bladder

372. Davidson body is used to determine:

    a.) Age

    b.) Race

    c.) Sex

    d.) Stature

373. Streak ovaries are seen in :

    a.) Turner Syndrome

    b.) Down Syndrome

    c.) Klinfelter Syndrome

    d.) Marfan's Syndrome

374. Cephalhematoma is a hemorrhage found between skull and periosteum in:

    a.) An Adult

    b.) A Child

c.) An old person aged about 60 and above

d.) A new born baby

375. Regarding human skull, which statement is correct:

   a.) Frontal eminences are larger in females

   b.) Occipital protuberances is more prominent in females

   c.) Parietal eminences are larger in females

   d.) a & c

376. True Hermaphroditism is when:

   a.) Testes/ovaries are absent

   b.) Testes and ovaries present in one individual

   c.) Presence of Ovaries

   d.) Presence of Testes

377. Krogman's formula is related to:

   a.) Race

   b.) Age

   c.) Stature

   d.) Sex

378. Best part for X-Ray to determine age of 7 years child:

   a.) Iliac

   b.) Wrist & Hand

   c.) Pelvis

   d.) Elbow

379. Palato print is commonly taken from which part of palate?

   a.) Anterior Part

   b.) Lateral wall

- c.) Medial wall
- d.) Posterior wall

380. Stature is determined by formula of:
    - a.) Locard's exchange principle
    - b.) Trotter and Gleser Formula
    - c.) Widmark Formula
    - d.) Hasse

381. Xenograft is transplantation of tissue:
    - a.) One part of body to another part of body
    - b.) From same species
    - c.) From different species
    - d.) All of the above

382. Under water autopsy of the heart is done in case of:
    - a.) Pneumothorax
    - b.) Air Embolism
    - c.) Myocardial Infraction
    - d.) Pulmonary Embolism

383. Hydrocution is:
    - a.) Immersion syndrome
    - b.) Hemolysis
    - c.) Dry drowning
    - d.) Wet drowning

384. The cause of death in immersion syndrome is:
    - a.) Ventricular Fibrillation
    - b.) Laryngeal Spasm

c.) Vagal Inhibition

d.) Asphyxia

385. Which one of the following is true about Immersion syndrome:

a.) Intense laryngeal spasm due to entry of water into nosopharynx a larynx.

b.) Due to sudden impact of the very cold water and causes death from cardiac arrest

c.) Circulatory Shock

d.) Water cross the alveolar membrane into the circulation

386. Fatal asphyxiation in child by putting food, toys into their mouth which obstruct the air passage is known as:

a.) Café coronary

b.) Crèche Coronary

c.) Gagging

d.) Choking

387. Tearing of the skin and tissue is known as:

a.) Laceration

b.) Contusion

c.) Abrasion

d.) Hemorrhage

388. Graze is a form of:

a.) Incised wound

b.) Abrasion

c.) Contusion

d.) Lacerated wound

Forensic Medicine

389. Chop Wound is caused by following, except;
    a.) Knife
    b.) Tomahawk
    c.) Axe
    d.) Hatchet

390. Stab wounds are fatal when:
    a.) Major pulmonary blood vessel has been cut
    b.) Self-inflicted
    c.) Penetration is about 1mm
    d.) Stab in stomach

391. Perforating wound is:
    a.) Weapons enter into the body producing only one wound.
    b.) Weapons after entering into one side of the body will come out through the other side.
    c.) Deep gaping wounds caused by a blow with the moderately sharp cutting edge of a heavy weapon.
    d.) Incision is a clean cut wound through the tissue, caused by a sharp-edged instrument.

392. Injury is fabricated if:
    a.) Location is easily reachable
    b.) Multiple shallow, non-penetrating cuts or fingernail abrasions.
    c.) Stab wound on chest
    d.) a & b

393. Kronlein shot is a very rare injury of the skull caused by:
    a.) Low-Velocity Bullet

b.) Medium-Velocity Bullet

c.) High-Velocity Bullet

d.) Any of the above

394. The distance of close shot is about:

   a.) 1-1.5 cm from skin

   b.) 10-20cm from skin

   c.) 2.5-7.5 cm from skin

   d.) 1 cm form skin

395. Bite mark is an example of:

   a.) Scratch Abrasion

   b.) Patterned Abrasion

   c.) Imprint Abrasion

   d.) Graze Abrasion

396. Bite marks can be found in case of:

   a.) Rape

   b.) Suicide

   c.) Traffic accident

   d.) Natural death

397. Blue color of contusion is due to:

   a.) De-oxyhemoglobin

   b.) Plasma

   c.) Hematoidin

   d.) Hemosiderin

398. Bruises seen on eyes, known as:

   a.) Red Eye

b.) Black Eye

c.) Bruised Eye

d.) Swollen Eye

399. The bluish-black to brown discoloration of the bruise is due to:

   a.) Hematoidin

   b.) Bilirubin

   c.) Hemosiderin

   d.) Biliverdin

400. Green Color of contusion is due to:

   a.) Biliverdin

   b.) Hematoidin

   c.) Hemosiderin

   d.) Bilirubin

401. Antemortem bruise is differentiated from postmortem bruise by:

   a.) Deoxyhemoglobin

   b.) Hematoidin

   c.) Capillary rupture with extravasation of blood

   d.) Presence of little amount of blood

402. Split laceration looked like:

   a.) Incised wound

   b.) Contusion

   c.) Abrasion

   d.) burns

403. Hesitation cuts are seen in case of:

   a.) Murder

b.) Suicide

c.) Accident

d.) Any of the above

404. Tissue bridges are seen in:

   a.) Abrasion

   b.) Contusion

   c.) Laceration

   d.) Stab wound

405. Incised wounds on genitalia:

   a.) Homicidal

   b.) Self-implicated

   c.) Accidental

   d.) Suicidal

406. Contact wound (made by firearm) shows:

   a.) Abrasion collar

   b.) Tattooing

   c.) Cruciate splitting

   d.) Burnt skin

407. Following are the feature of gunshot injury in skull, except:

   a.) Entrance wound in beveled in the inner table

   b.) Entrance wound beveled in the outer table

   c.) Exit wound beveled in the outer table

   d.) Exit wound beveled in the inner table

408. In firearm injury, there is boning, blackening, tattooing around the wound, and, is circular in shape; the injury is:

a.) Close shot entry

b.) Close contact exit

c.) Contact wound

d.) Distant shot

409. Molotov Cocktail is:

a.) Mixtures of alcohol

b.) Petrol Bombs

c.) A Special Drink

d.) A case of person named as Molotov

410. Which one is false about grievous hurt:

a.) Loss of one kidney

b.) Loss of hearing from one ear

c.) Fracture in hand

d.) Loss of one eye

411. Following increase the risk of bone fractures:

a.) Exercise

b.) Lack of sleep

c.) Tobacco and Nicotine

d.) Gender

412. How much blood is loss when the size of clot is of fist size:

a.) 10-50 ml

b.) 100-150 ml

c.) 200-300 ml

d.) 400-500 ml

413. Commonest cause of pulmonary embolism is:

a.) Fat

b.) Amniotic fluid

c.) Thrombus

d.) Air

414. What is the source of energy if person eat nothing since 7 days:

a.) Acetone

b.) Acetoacetate

c.) Glucose

d.) Amino acids

415. If person eat and drink nothing then he will die in:

a.) 1 week

b.) 2-5 days

c.) 2-3 week

d.) Few hours

416. Last one to disappear in starvation, is:

a.) Fat around abdomen

b.) Buccal fat

c.) Fat around the eyes

d.) Fat in the mesentery

417. In blast injury, most common organ affected:

a.) Eardrum

b.) Stomach

c.) Lungs

d.) Liver

418. Which of these factors influences healing of a wound?

a.) Diabetes

b.) Food

c.) Malnutrition

d.) a & c

419. Best prognostic indicator for head injured patients is:

a.) GCS (Glasgow Coma Scale)

b.) CT (Computerized Tomography) Scan

c.) History of patient

d.) Age

420. Antegrade amnesia is seen in:

a.) Post Traumatic Head Injury

b.) Drug Induced

c.) Electroconvulsive Therapy

d.) Stroke

421. Paradoxical undressing is seen in:

a.) Hyperthermia

b.) Hypothermia

c.) Tranvestism

d.) Immersion syndrome

422. Sweating is absent in:

a.) Immersion syndrome

b.) Heat stroke

c.) Heat cramps

d.) Hyperthermia

423. According to 'rule of 9', perineum burns constitute:

Forensic Medicine

   a.) 1%
   b.) 25%
   c.) 10%
   d.) 50%

424. Heba classification is used for:

   a.) Burn
   b.) Age
   c.) Stature
   d.) Death

425. According to heba's classification burn are classified into:

   a.) 1
   b.) 2
   c.) 3
   d.) 4

426. Parkland formula is used for resuscitation of burns is for:

   a.) Lactated Ringer's (LR)
   b.) Normal Saline
   c.) Glucose Saline
   d.) 25% Dextrose

427. Muils and Barclays formula is for:

   a.) Anthropometry
   b.) Stature
   c.) Colloid based resuscitation in major burns
   d.) Sex determination

428. In the case of burning, blister burst after:

a.) 2-3 days

b.) 5-6 days

c.) 8-10 days

d.) 11-12 days

429. Blister Formation occurred in burn after:

a.) 1 hour

b.) 2 hour

c.) 3 hour

d.) 4 hour

430. Primary impact injury must commonly seen in :

a.) Head

b.) Throax

c.) Eyes

d.) Abdomen

431. Most common organ injured in penetrating injury of the abdomen:

a.) Liver

b.) Spleen

c.) Stomach

d.) Small intestine

432. Someone else's fertilized egg is implanted in another woman, this is known as:

a.) Traditional Surrogacy

b.) Gestational Surrogacy

c.) Primary Surrogacy

d.) All of the above

Forensic Medicine

433. Atavism is inheritance of feature of:

    a.) Father

    b.) Grandmother

    c.) Mother

    d.) Brother

434. Hymen can be rupture by all; except:

    a.) Sexual intercourse

    b.) Surgical operation

    c.) Sanitary Tampons

    d.) Exercise

435. The Common Site and Traumatic rupture of hymen is seen on the:

    a.) Anterior Aspect

    b.) Posterior Aspect

    c.) Lateral Aspect

    d.) Posterio-Lateral Aspect

436. In following situation Hymen may not rupture after rape:

    a.) Penetration was not full

    b.) Hymen is tough, fleshy and elastic

    c.) In deflorated women

    d.) All of the above

437. Most common cause of erectile dysfunction:

    a.) Psychological

    b.) Drug induced

    c.) Alcohol

    d.) Diabetes

438. Test for vaginal cells in case of rape is:

   a.) Alternate light source

   b.) Acid phosphatase test

   c.) Lugol's Iodine

   d.) Benzidine Test

439. In Algolagnia:

   a.) Person gets sexual gratification by infliction of pain or physical cruelty.

   b.) The person gets sexual gratification by inducing his wife to have sexual intercourse with another man.

   c.) Person gets sexual gratification by collecting opposite sex clothes.

   d.) Person wears opposite sex clothes to get sexual gratification.

440. Lust murder is an extreme form of:

   a.) Troilism

   b.) Masochism

   c.) Algolagnia

   d.) Lesbianism

441. Buccal Coitus is related to:

   a.) Oral Intercourse

   b.) Anal Intercourse

   c.) Sexual Intercourse

   d.) Rape

442. No spermatozoa recovered from semen, in case of:

   a.) Azoospermia

   b.) Vasectomy

Forensic Medicine

    c.) Old age

    d.) All of the above

443. The stains on the clothes can be identified conclusively as semen by :

    a.) Acid Phosphatase Test

    b.) Barberio's Test

    c.) Spermatozoa

    d.) All Of the Above

444. 'Falanga' is:

    a.) Electric current for torture

    b.) Pulling of hair

    c.) Hitting the feet with stick

    d.) Self-inflicted injury

445. Which body fluid is not responsible for the transmission of HIV:

    a.) Semen

    b.) Breast Milk

    c.) Tears

    d.) Blood

446. HLA typing is useful in:

    a.) Disputed paternity

    b.) Organ transplant

    c.) a & b

    d.) Dactylography

447. The term "Halitosis" denotes which one of the following:

    a.) Hearing Impairment

    b.) Vision Impairment

    c.) Bad Breath

d.) Excessive Sweating

448. Disease of which among the following are included in degenerative disease?

a.) Heart

b.) Joint

c.) Nervous system

d.) All of the above

449. Antibiotics in high dose can cause the suppression of synthesis of which one of the following vitamins in human body?

a.) Vitamin A

b.) Biotin

c.) Vitamin K

d.) Vitamin B

450. Bowman's Glands are located in the:

a.) Anterior pituitary

b.) Olfactory epithelium of our nose

c.) Proximal end or uriniferous tubules

d.) In hand

451. Human RBC placed in 1.5% NaCl solution will:

a.) Burst

b.) Shrink

c.) No effect

d.) Extended

452. When blood of one individual is mixed with another individual's blood/serum, clotting of RBC may occur because of:

a.) Antigen-Antibody Reaction

b.) Antibody-Antibody Reaction

c.) Antigen-Antigen Reaction

d.) None of the above

453. Progesterone is secreted by:

a.) Thymus

b.) Thyroid

c.) Testis

d.) Corpus luteum

454. Injury of which of these nerve cause vocal cord paralysis?

a.) External Laryngeal

b.) Recurrent Laryngeal

c.) Internal Laryngeal

d.) Superior Laryngeal

455. In deltoid paralysis, which nerve is involve:

a.) Musculocutaneous Nerve

b.) Circumflex Nerve

c.) Radial Nerve

d.) Axillary Nerve

456. Lockwood ligament is found in:

a.) Temporomandibular Joint (TMJ)

b.) Pharynx

c.) Larynx

d.) Orbit

457. What if ligament is torn?

- a.) Bones will move freely at joint
- b.) Bones will never be fixed
- c.) Bones will fix automatically
- d.) Bone less movable at joint and will pain

458. The end of long bones contains following cartilage:
    - a.) Calcified cartilage
    - b.) Hyaline Cartilage
    - c.) Fibrous Cartilage
    - d.) Elastic Cartilage

459. Kuffer's cells occur in:
    - a.) Liver
    - b.) Kidney
    - c.) Spleen
    - d.) Brain

460. Following part of the body secrets the hormone secretin:
    - a.) Ileum
    - b.) Rectum
    - c.) Duodenum
    - d.) Esophagus

461. Which one of the following is the type of joint between the skull bones of human:
    - a.) Cartilaginous Joint
    - b.) Hinge Joint
    - c.) Fibrous Joint
    - d.) Synovial Joint

Forensic Medicine

462. Which of the following may be used to estimate the age of person at time of his/her death with regard to skeletonized human remains:
    a.) Adipocere formation
    b.) Superimposition
    c.) Epiphyseal union
    d.) Hypostasis

463. Fingernails are made up of:
    a.) Potassium
    b.) Calcium
    c.) Keratin
    d.) Sodium

464. Northern blot test is used for:
    a.) DNA Analysis
    b.) RNA Analysis
    c.) Protein Analysis
    d.) Enzyme Analysis

465. Telefona is:
    a.) Beating on both ears
    b.) Beating on back
    c.) Beating on soles
    d.) Beating on hands

466. A person found dead in his room. He was hanged by rope from sealing fan. Body has Dribbling of saliva, noncontinuous ligature mark and dilated eyes. His fists were clenched. This is case of:
    a.) Suicide

b.) Homicide

c.) Accidental

d.) Lynching

467. If a dead body of human is floating on the surface of river in month of May. The person has been dead from:

   a.) 1 days

   b.) 2-3 days

   c.) 1-2 weeks

   d.) 15-20 days

468. Jaundice is caused by:

   a.) Excessive collection of Calcium in body

   b.) Excessive Protein in the body

   c.) Excessive level of Vitamins in body

   d.) Excessive level of Bilirubin in the body

469. Maximum drugs are metabolized in:

   a.) Kidney

   b.) Brain

   c.) Small Intestine

   d.) Liver

470. Movement of food in intestine and circular muscle in the stomach is:

   a.) Digestion

   b.) Peristalsis

   c.) Active motion

   d.) Constipation

471. If food is found in the small intestine, but stomach is empty then death occurred:

   a.) 1-2 hours after meal

   b.) 10-12 hours after meal

   c.) 4-6 hours after meal

   d.) Few minutes after meal

472. Tonsil is a:

   a.) Muscular Tissue

   b.) Lymphoid Tissue

   c.) Connective Tissue

   d.) Epithelial Tissue

473. Diuretics causes loss of:

   a.) Sodium

   b.) Potassium

   c.) Calcium

   d.) Iron

474. A child teeth stained permanently after exposure from:

   a.) Diphenyl Hydantoin

   b.) Diphenhydramine

   c.) Digoxin

   d.) Doxycycline

475. According to Dupuytren's classification blister formation is graded as:

   a.) I Degree

   b.) II Degree

   c.) III Degree

d.) IV Degree

476. The identification of dead body can be done by:

    a.) Putrefied body

    b.) Place of Occurrence

    c.) Laundry & Tailor marks on cloths

    d.) None

477. The situation in which the blood separates into distinct units is known as:

    a.) Ophthalmologic Changes

    b.) Trucking

    c.) Dilation

    d.) Contraction

478. Which insects are the first to appear on the dead body:

    a.) Beetles

    b.) Ants

    c.) Flies

    d.) Mites

479. In which stage house-flies begin to appear and deposit eggs:

    a.) Fresh Stage

    b.) Post-Decay Stage

    c.) Bloated Stage

    d.) Decay Stage

480. Corpse appears normal on the outside, but is starting to decompose and insects starts laying eggs:

    a.) Fresh Stage

b.) Active Decay Stage

c.) Post Decay Stage

d.) Decay Stage

481. Which stage begins with the splitting of the skin to allow the gases to escape?

   a.) Rigor Mortis

   b.) Decay Stage

   c.) Bloated Stage

   d.) Post-decay Stage

482. Which stage occurs due to activity of bacteria which produce gases inside the body?

   a.) Rigor Mortis

   b.) Decay Stage

   c.) Bloated Stage

   d.) Post-decay Stage

483. Cyanosis occurs when the concentration of reduced hemoglobin exceeds:

   a.) 10 gm %

   b.) 5 gm%

   c.) 15 gm%

   d.) 2 gm%

484. Cyanosis commonly known as:

   a.) Oxygenated disease

   b.) Decreased hemoglobin

   c.) Blue hands or feet

d.) Cyan

485. Cyanosis is caused by:
    a.) An increased concentration of reduced hemoglobin
    b.) A decreased concentration of oxyhemoglobin
    c.) Hypoxia
    d.) A decreased concentration of hemoglobin

486. Commonest cause of hemobilia is:
    a.) Gall stones
    b.) Trauma
    c.) Cholangitis
    d.) Hepatoma

487. In India, Splenectomy is most commonly performed for:
    a.) Hydatid cyst
    b.) Carcinoma thyroid
    c.) Trauma
    d.) Portal hypertension

488. Larvae are voracious feeders in following stage of the fly cycle:
    a.) Ist Instar
    b.) IInd Instar
    c.) IIIrd Instar
    d.) IVth Instar

489. If larvae are found in stage IInd and IIIrd then person has been dead from:
    a.) 2-4 days
    b.) 8-10 days

Forensic Medicine

   c.) 10-14 days

   d.) 2 Weeks

490. Following blowflies don't have much forensic value, as it is unclear whether they have just arrived at the scene or have developed on the body:

   a.) Adult

   b.) Juvenile

   c.) Larvae

   d.) Pupae

491. Rule of Thumb determines:

   a.) Height

   b.) Length of wound

   c.) Postmortem Estimation

   d.) Fingerprints

492. Formula of Rule Of Thumb:

   a.) Stature x PMI/48

   b.) Heat Loss = 1^0C per hour

   c.) Temperature of body x TOD/24

   d.) Stature =PMI/48

493. Glaister equation:

   a.) Calculates the structure of bone

   b.) Calculates the hours passing after death

   c.) Calculates the stature

   d.) Calculates the total fractures in body

494. Glaister equation is:

a.) 98.7⁰F - Rectal Temperature /1.5⁰C per hour = PMI

b.) 98.7⁰F – the dead body temperature

c.) 98.7⁰F/1.5⁰C per hour

d.) Rectal temperature/1.5⁰C per hour

495. In antemortem tooth loss or extraction, the alveolus is:

a.) Smooth

b.) Sharp and feathered

c.) Does not show any injury

d.) May have a regular appearance

496. Infanticide is:

a.) Killing of child aged about 11-15 year

b.) Killing of child

c.) Killing of newly born child within one year

d.) Killing of 0-5 year old child

497. How many bones are in the skeleton of an infant?

a.) 206

b.) 300

c.) Skeleton are made up of cartilage

d.) 250

498. Direct impact on bone may produce

a.) Spiral fracture

b.) Transverse fracture

c.) Oblique fracture

d.) Avulsion fracture

499. The body digest food within:

a.) 5-10 hours

b.) 7-8 hours

c.) 10-12 hours

d.) 24-72 hours

500. Othello syndrome related to:

   a.) Person feels that his/her partner has been disloyal.

   b.) Person believes that everyone, every matter concerning him/her.

   c.) He/she belief that he is suffering from dangerous disease.

   d.) Person does not believe in his/her existence.

Answer-Sheet

Forensic Medicine

1	a	2	c	3	b	4	b	5	a	6	c	7	b	8	a	9	e	10	b
11	d	12	a	13	c	14	c	15	a	16	c	17	d	18	b	19	d	20	b
21	b	22	d	23	c	24	c	25	d	26	b	27	d	28	a	29	c	30	a
31	a	32	b	33	d	34	d	35	c	36	c	37	c	38	a	39	a	40	b
41	c	42	b	43	a	44	c	45	d	46	a	47	b	48	a	49	b	50	a
51	d	52	a	53	d	54	a	55	b	56	a	57	d	58	a	59	c	60	d
61	b	62	c	63	b	64	c	65	a	66	d	67	d	68	a	69	b	70	b
71	a	72	b	73	a	74	c	75	a	76	d	77	d	78	c	79	c	80	c
81	a	82	b	83	c	84	a	85	b	86	b	87	b	88	a	89	c	90	c
91	a	92	d	93	c	94	c	95	d	96	d	97	c	98	d	99	c	100	c
101	b	102	d	103	b	104	d	105	b	106	c	107	a	108	c	109	a	110	d
111	b	112	d	113	d	114	b	115	d	116	b	117	b	118	b	119	d	120	d
121	b	122	c	123	c	124	d	125	b	126	a	127	b	128	d	129	c	130	a
131	b	132	a	133	b	134	b	135	b	136	d	137	a	138	a	139	b	140	a
141	d	142	a	143	b	144	d	145	c	146	a	147	a	148	b	149	a	150	c
151	b	152	d	153	b	154	c	155	d	156	b	157	a	158	b	159	c	160	c
161	b	162	d	163	a	164	a	165	a	166	c	167	a	168	b	169	d	170	b
171	a	172	c	173	b	174	c	175	c	176	c	177	a	178	d	179	a	180	d
181	d	182	c	183	c	184	b	185	a	186	c	187	a	188	b	189	a	190	b
191	c	192	c	193	c	194	b	195	d	196	a	197	b	198	c	199	d	200	a
201	b	202	b	203	a	204	a	205	b	206	c	207	a	208	d	209	a	210	d
211	c	212	d	213	c	214	a	215	a	216	a	217	a	218	b	219	c	220	d
221	a	222	b	223	b	224	a	225	a	226	e	227	b	228	d	229	a	230	b
231	b	232	c	233	b	234	d	235	a	236	c	237	c	238	d	239	c	240	c
241	b	242	a	243	b	244	b	245	a	246	b	247	c	248	a	249	b	250	b
251	c	252	e	253	b	254	a	255	c	256	b	257	b	258	a	259	d	260	b
261	c	262	d	263	c	264	d	265	b	266	a	267	a	268	b	269	a	270	b
271	a	272	b	273	c	274	d	275	b	276	c	277	d	278	c	279	d	280	d

Forensic Medicine

281	b	282	d	283	c	284	a	285	a	286	b	287	d	288	c	289	a	290	a
291	c	292	d	293	b	294	b	295	c	296	a	297	b	298	c	299	d	300	b
301	b	302	b	303	c	304	c	305	b	306	d	307	b	308	a	309	b	310	c
311	d	312	a	313	d	314	b	315	c	316	d	317	b	318	c	319	d	320	a
321	d	322	b	323	e	324	a	325	a	326	b	327	b	328	a	329	d	330	c
331	a	332	c	333	a	334	b	335	d	336	b	337	a	338	b	339	e	340	c
341	a	342	a	343	b	344	d	345	b	346	c	347	d	348	a	349	a	350	c
351	b	352	c	353	c	354	c	355	b	356	d	357	a	358	b	359	b	360	b
361	a	362	b	363	b	364	d	365	d	366	a	367	b	368	a	369	d	370	c
371	a	372	c	373	a	374	d	375	d	376	b	377	d	378	b	379	a	380	b
381	c	382	b	383	a	384	c	385	b	386	b	387	a	388	b	389	a	390	a
391	a	392	d	393	c	394	c	395	b	396	a	397	a	398	b	399	c	400	a
401	c	402	a	403	b	404	c	405	a	406	c	407	b	408	a	409	b	410	c
411	c	412	d	413	c	414	a	415	c	416	b	417	a	418	d	419	a	420	a
421	b	422	c	423	a	424	a	425	d	426	a	427	c	428	b	429	a	430	c
431	a	432	b	433	b	434	d	435	d	436	d	437	a	438	c	439	a	440	c
441	a	442	d	443	d	444	c	445	c	446	c	447	c	448	d	449	b	450	b
451	b	452	a	453	d	454	b	455	d	456	d	457	d	458	b	459	a	460	c
461	c	462	c	463	c	464	b	465	a	466	a	467	b	468	d	469	d	470	b
471	c	472	b	473	b	474	d	475	b	476	c	477	b	478	c	479	d	480	a
481	b	482	c	483	b	484	c	485	d	486	b	487	c	488	c	489	a	490	a
491	c	492	b	493	b	494	a	495	b	496	c	497	b	498	b	499	d	500	a

Forensic Medicine

Notes

Part- 2

Forensic Toxicology

Forensic Toxicology

1. The term Toxicology is derived from the world:
   a.) Toxic
   b.) Toxicon
   c.) Toxico
   d.) Toxics

2. The Father of Forensic Toxicology is:
   a.) Karl Landsteiner
   b.) Amboise Pare
   c.) Mathieu J. B. Orfila
   d.) Manu

3. The toxicology maxims *"The Dose makes the Poison"* is said by:
   a.) Karl Landsteiner
   b.) Amboise Pare
   c.) Mathieu J. B. Orfila
   d.) Paracelsus

4. Study of toxic substance produced by living organism in the human body and their effect is known as:
   a.) Toxinology
   b.) Toxicology
   c.) Forensic Medicine
   d.) Clinical Toxicology

5. Any type of natural or synthetic matter/substance which is used to produce physiological and psychological effects in livings is called as:
   a.) Poison
   b.) Drug
   c.) Medicine
   d.) Antidote

6. What is the ratio of poison and drug?
   a.) 5:10
   b.) 2:5

c.) 10:10

d.) 1:10

7. Under NDPS Act following drugs are included, except:

a.) Alcohol

b.) Opium

c.) Amphetamine

d.) Hashish

8. Any substance in any form, is capable of producing detrimental effects on living organism is known as:

a.) Poison

b.) Drug

c.) Medicine

d.) Antidote

9. Which drug is imported under a name of another drug, or it is an imitation of another drug which can deceive the person is known as:

a.) Adulterated Drug

b.) Misbranded Drug

c.) Spurious Drug

d.) Illicit Drug

10. Soluble toxic protein released from gram positive or gram negative bacteria is known as:

a.) Endotoxin

b.) Exotoxin

c.) Enterotoxin

d.) Poison

11. These are heat stable lipopolysaccharide complex of the outer membrane of the cell wall of gram negative bacteria:

a.) Exotoxin

b.) Enterotoxin

c.) Endotoxin

d.) Poison

12. These are toxins produced by bacteria which is specific for intestinal cells:
    a.) Exotoxin
    b.) Enterotoxin
    c.) Endotoxin
    d.) Poison

13. Poisoning having Local action only:
    a) Sulphuric Acid
    b) Arsenic
    c) Oxalic Acid
    d) Carbon Monoxide

14. Chemicals have specific targets in the body:
    a.) Few does have targets, others are nonspecific
    b.) Depends on Immune System
    c.) Depends on the route of exposure
    d.) Chemicals decide after entering into the body

15. Synergism comes from the Greek word, which is:
    a.) Synergist
    b.) Synerg
    c.) Synergos
    d.) Antidote

16. A substance which is used to neutralize or counteract the effect of poison is called?
    a.) Medicine
    b.) Chemical Neutralizer
    c.) Antibiotic
    d.) Antidote

17. Drugs which are alkaline in nature are called_____.
    a.) Poison
    b.) Alkali

- c.) Basic Drug
- d.) Acidic Drug

18. Drugs which are acidic in nature are called_____.
    - a.) Poison
    - b.) Alkali
    - c.) Basic Drug
    - d.) Acidic Drug

19. The substance which act chemically to form a nontoxic compound by forming insoluble compounds with the poison are known as-
    - a.) Universal Antidote
    - b.) Physiological Antidote
    - c.) Chemical Antidote
    - d.) Mechanical Antidote

20. Universal Antidote for unknown Poison is:
    - a.) Powedered Activated Charcoal: Magnesium Oxide: Tannic Acid
    - b.) Magnesium Oxide: Tinned Juice: Alkalis
    - c.) Sulphur: Carbolic Acid: Lime
    - d.) Luke Warm Water

21. Universal antidote prepared from common household articles:
    - a.) Wall Scraping: Tea: Toasted Bread
    - b.) Soil : Strong Black Tea: Charred Toasted Bread
    - c.) Wall Scraping: Strong Black Tea: Soap Solution
    - d.) Wall Scraping: Strong Black Tea: Charred Toasted Bread

22. The composition of universal antidote includes two parts of:
    - a.) Magnesium oxide
    - b.) Tannic Acid
    - c.) Powder Activated Charcoal
    - d.) All of the above

23. Activated Charcoal is an Example for:
    - a.) Universal Antidote

b.) Physiological Antidote

c.) Chemical Antidote

d.) Mechanical Antidote

24. Activated charcoal is prepared by:

a.) Burning wood

b.) Bacteria

c.) Chemical synthesis

d.) Artificial technique

25. Activated Charcoal is Ineffective in Poisoning of:

a.) Methyl Alcohol

b.) Ethyl Alcohol

c.) Arsenic

d.) All of the above

26. Instead of Charcoal this can be also used:

a.) Raw Egg

b.) Mashed Potatoes in water

c.) Warm Milk

d.) Luke Warm Water

27. Which following poison has no antidote?

a.) Mustard Gas

b.) Hydrofluoric Acid

c.) Batrachotoxin

d.) Sulfur Dioxide

e.) Dimethylmercury

f.) All of the above

28. Atropine and Pralidoxime are antidotes for:

a.) Blood Agent

b.) Nerve Agent

c.) Blister agent

Forensic Toxicology

   d.) Choking agent

29. In suspected chronic poisoning, the following specimen should be collected:

   a.) Hairs

   b.) Nails

   c.) Skin (sole of feet and palm of hand)

   d.) Ends of the long bone.

   e.) All of the above

30. A person gets unconscious, excessive salivation, constricted pupils and fasciculation muscles, treatment started with:

   a.) Lukewarm water

   b.) Atropine

   c.) Adrenaline

   d.) All of the above

31. All statements are true about symptoms of blister agent, except:

   a.) Skin, eye, and mucosal pain and irritation.

   b.) Painful breathing or shortness of breath.

   c.) Mild respiratory distress to marked airway damage.

   d.) Blister agents are denser than air.

32. Following are mineral acids, except:

   a.) Sulphuric Acid

   b.) Nitric Acid

   c.) Hydrochloric Acid

   d.) Carbolic Acid.

33. Which nut contains Cyanide?

   a.) Cashews

   b.) Pistachios

   c.) Walnuts

   d.) Bitter Almonds

34. PAPP (Para-aminopropiophenone) is used in the treatment of one of the following poison:
   a.) Alcohol poisoning
   b.) Barbiturate poisoning
   c.) Opiate poisoning
   d.) Cyanide poisoning

35. Which is the most deadly Poison?
   a.) Sulphuric Acid
   b.) Arsenic
   c.) Botulinum Toxin
   d.) Carbon Monoxide

36. Which Bacteria Produced Botulinum Toxin?
   a.) Streptococcus Pyogenes
   b.) Mycobacterium Tuberculosis
   c.) Clostridium Botulinum
   d.) Acinetobacter Baumannii

37. Botox is known to tighten the skin and reduce wrinkles. Which Toxin is being used in Botox?
   a.) Sulphuric Acid
   b.) Arsenic
   c.) Botulinum Toxin
   d.) Carbon Monoxide

38. This is most deadliest poison:
   a.) Botulinum Toxin
   b.) VX
   c.) Maitotoxin
   d.) Polonium
   e.) All of the above

39. Polonium is a:
   a.) Gaseous Element

Forensic Toxicology

- b.) Liquid Element
- c.) solid element
- d.) Radioactive Element

40. A potential lethal dose of Polonium-210 is:
    - a.) 0.1 Sieverts
    - b.) 10 Sieverts
    - c.) 5 Sieverts
    - d.) 100 Sieverts

41. O-ethyl S-diisopropylaminomethyl methylphosphonothiolate is chemical name of following Poison:
    - a.) Botulinum Toxin
    - b.) VX
    - c.) Maitotoxin
    - d.) Polonium

42. VX was discovered by:
    - a.) Gerhard Schrader
    - b.) Paracelsus
    - c.) Ranaji Ghosh
    - d.) a & c

43. Lethal dose of Batrachotoxin (BTX) is:
    - a.) 10g/kg
    - b.) 0.2g/kg
    - c.) 3g/kg
    - d.) 1g/kg

44. Batrachotoxin (BTX) is produced by:
    - a.) Chemical synthesis
    - b.) By certain species of frogs
    - c.) Bacteria
    - d.) Plant

45. Maitotoxin is produced by:

a.) Gambierdiscus Toxicus

b.) Parachlorella Kessleri

c.) Mytilus galloprovincialis

d.) Ruditapes Philippinarum

46. Lethal dose of Maitotoxin is:

a.) 1g/kg

b.) 0.2g/kg

c.) 3g/kg

d.) 50ng/kg

47. Powder form of Cyanide is known as:

a.) Hydrogen Cyanide

b.) Potassium Cyanide

c.) Hydrocyanic Acid

d.) None

48. In which one of the following of the organ toxically significant level of cyanide may be found even after advanced decomposition of Body?

a.) Lever

b.) Spleen

c.) Heart

d.) Kidney

49. Who first of all described the association between chemical exposure and cancer?

a.) Percivall Pott

b.) Paracelsus

c.) Mathieu Orfila

d.) Ambroise Pare

50. Poisoning from Acetaminophen/Paracetamol can cause damage to:

a.) Bones

b.) Heart

c.) Lungs

d.) Liver

51. Some Poisons Impart characteristic colorations in body which is known as:

    a.) Body color

    b.) Postmortem Changes

    c.) Postmortem Lividity

    d.) Ante-mortem

52. Brick red color of post mortem lividity is seen in poisoning due to:

    a.) Lead

    b.) Arsenic

    c.) Cyanide

    d.) Carbon Monoxide

53. Cherry pink color of post mortem lividity is seen in poisoning due to:

    a.) Carbon Monoxide

    b.) Hydrogen Sulphide

    c.) Lead

    d.) Cyanide

54. Greenish Blue coolr of post mortem lividity is seen in poisoning due to:

    a.) Lead

    b.) Hydrogen Sulphide

    c.) Cyanide

    d.) Carbon Monoxide

55. Red (boiled Lobster) color of post mortem lividity is seen in poisoning due to:

    a.) Lead

    b.) Hydrogen Sulphide

    c.) Boric Acid

    d.) Carbon Monoxide

56. Brown color of post mortem lividity and garlic odor in stomach is seen in poisoning due to:

a.) Phosphorus

b.) Hydrogen Sulphide

c.) Cyanide

d.) Carbon Monoxide

57. Jaundice/Yellow color of post mortem lividity is seen in these poisonings, Except:

a.) Mushrooms

b.) Nitro Compounds

c.) Cyanide

d.) Picric Acid

58. Red-Brown color of post mortem lividity is seen in poisoning due to:

a.) Nitrites

b.) Silver Salts

c.) Cyanide

d.) Carbon Monoxide

59. Blue-Gray color of post mortem lividity is seen in poisoning due to:

a.) Phosphorus

b.) Silver Salts

c.) Cyanide

d.) Carbon Monoxide

60. Danbury tremor is seen in:

a.) Carbon Monoxide

b.) Lead poisoning

c.) Arsenic poisoning

d.) Mercury poisoning

61. Mad hatter is seen in:

a.) Carbon Monoxide

b.) Lead poisoning

c.) Arsenic poisoning

d.) Mercury poisoning

Forensic Toxicology

62. Acrodynia disease is caused by:
    a.) Carbon Monoxide
    b.) Mercury poisoning
    c.) Lead poisoning
    d.) Arsenic poisoning

63. How Danbury tremor begins and progress in body?
    a.) It begins in the hand and progresses to lips, tongue, arms and legs.
    b.) It begins in the head and progresses to lips, tongue, arms and legs.
    c.) It begins from the face and progresses to lips, tongue, arms and legs.
    d.) It begins in the legs and progresses to hips, Stomach, Chest and Head.

64. A toxic substance produced by biological system is referred as a _____:
    a.) Xenobiotic
    b.) Toxin
    c.) Toxic
    d.) Poison

65. Prolonged muscle relaxation after succinylcholine is an example of :
    a.) Idiosyncratic Reaction
    b.) Reaction related to a genetic increase in the activity of a liver enzyme
    c.) IGE- mediated allergic reaction
    d.) Immune complex reaction

66. Red colored hypostasis is seen in death because of following poison:
    a.) Carbon Monoxide Poisoning
    b.) Due to Cold
    c.) Cyanide Poisoning
    d.) Because of All

67. In case of acute carbon monoxide poisoning, coma and death with red color occurred at a carboxy haemoglobin level of:

a.) 30-40%
b.) 50-60%
c.) 60-70%
d.) 70-80%

68. Skin rash, confusion with lethargy, painful peripheral neuropathy and Alopecia are usually with lethargy are seen in poisoning with:
    a.) Thallium
    b.) Arsenic
    c.) Mercury
    d.) Nickel

69. A person found on railway platform. He was talking irrelevant. He was having dry mouth with hot skin, dilated pupils, staggering gait and slurred speech. The most probable diagnosis is:
    a.) Alcohol intoxication
    b.) Carbamates poisoning
    c.) Organophosphorous poisoning
    d.) Dhatura poisoning

70. Coma cocktail Consist of Following, except:
    a.) Naloxene
    b.) Thiamine
    c.) Pyridoxine
    d.) Flumazenil

71. Which one of the arsenic compounds causes hemolysis?
    a.) Arsenic Trioxide (As_2O_3)
    b.) Arsenic Pentaoxide (As_2O_5)
    c.) Arsine (AsH_3)
    d.) All of the Above

72. Antidote for Arsenic Poisoning:
    a.) Dimercaprol
    b.) EDTA

Forensic Toxicology

    c.) Penicillamine

    d.) Sodium Nitrate

73. In Chronic Poisoning red pigmentation on skin occurs due to:

    a.) Mercury

    b.) Antimony

    c.) Arsenic

    d.) Lead

74. Bloody Rice Water Diarrhea occurs in Poisoning from:

    a.) Mercury

    b.) Antimony

    c.) Arsenic

    d.) Lead

75. Marsh Test is used for detection of

    a.) Arsenic

    b.) Copper

    c.) Nitric Acid

    d.) CO

76. Freshly precipitated iron oxide can neutralizes:

    a.) Oxalic acid

    b.) Alkalis

    c.) Arsenic

    d.) Acids

77. Delayed rigor mortis occurs in case of:

    a.) Carbon Monoxide

    b.) Lead

    c.) Arsenic

    d.) Copper

78. Poison which can be detected from burnt bone:

    a.) Arsenic

b.) Mercury

c.) Chromium

d.) Lead

79. A Yellow stain on the paper in Gutzeit Test indicates the presence of

   a.) Mercury Poisoning

   b.) Antimony Poisoning

   c.) Arsenic Poisoning

   d.) Lead Poisoning

80. Gutzeit Method is used for the extraction of:

   a.) Inorganic Poison

   b.) Volatile Inorganic Poison

   c.) Volatile Organic Poison

   d.) Gaseous Poison

81. Arsenic can be detected in presence of Antimony by which test?

   a.) Reinsch Test

   b.) Ammonium Molybdate Test

   c.) Marsh's Test

   d.) Gutzeit Test

82. All of these would show accumulation of arsenic in case of acute arsenic poisoning, except-

   a.) Liver

   b.) Bone marrow

   c.) Skin

   d.) Brain

83. Mee's lines are characteristics of-

   a.) Mercury poisoning

   b.) Barbiturate poisoning

   c.) Arsenic Poisoning

   d.) Dhatura Poisoning

84. Fatty Yellow Liver is seen in poisoning with:

Forensic Toxicology

a.) Arsenic

b.) Alcohol

c.) Mercury

d.) Organophosphorus

85. Golden hair is seen in:

a.) Carbon monoxide poisoning

b.) Phosphorus poisoning

c.) Barbiturates poisoning

d.) Arsenic Poisoning

86. Which one of the following is used to preserve animal tissue, strengthen wood, carpet and other materials, but long exposure can lead to Leukemia and other varieties of cancer, ingesting a small amount of liquid can cause death.

a.) Acetaldehyde

b.) Formaldehyde and Formic Acid

c.) Pyridine

d.) Acetic acid

87. In methyl alcohol poisoning, there is central nervous system depression, cardiac depression and optic nerve atrophy. These effects are produced due to:

a.) Formaldehyde and Formic Acid

b.) Acetaldehyde

c.) Pyridine

d.) Acetic acid

88. The average rate of alcohol elimination in breath per hour is:

a.) 3 μg/dl

b.) 6 μg/dl

c.) 15 μg/dl

d.) 30 μg/dl

89. Pyknometer method is used to estimate which of the following property of alcoholic beverage?

a.) Methanol content

b.) Ethyl alcohol content

c.) Volatile poison content

d.) Alcohol Content

90. Which one of the following is used to produce Toddy?

a.) Rice

b.) Wheat

c.) Mahua

d.) Palm

91. A toxicant produced by an animal is called

a.) Animal Toxin

b.) poison

c.) Venom

d.) Mycotoxin

92. Sodium Azide (Na_2N^3) has a mechanism of toxicity similar to:

a.) Cyanide

b.) Carbon Monoxide

c.) THC

d.) Benzene

93. Sodium Azide (Na_2N^3) is used in

a.) Refrigeration

b.) Air cooling

c.) Painting

d.) Air bags of car

94. Organs of dead body have an odor of bitter almond. Which volatile is poison?

a.) Phenol

b.) Chloroform

c.) Hydrocyanic acid

d.) Acetone

95. What volatile poison can be suspected as the reason of the poisoning in which Urine has a dark green color?

   a.) Phenol

   b.) Acetone

   c.) Ethanol

   d.) Methanol

96. The urine is turned olive or black olive due to poisoning by:

   a.) Copper sulphate

   b.) Isoamyl alcohol

   c.) Phenol

   d.) Iodoform

97. The color of stomach contents will turn black due to this poison:

   a.) Oxalic Acid

   b.) Isoamyl alcohol

   c.) Phenol

   d.) Iodoform

98. Which one of the following poisoning may cause pink color stomach wall:

   a.) Nitric Acid

   b.) Copper sulphate

   c.) Soneryl

   d.) Amytal

99. The color of stomach contents will turn bluish green due to this poison:

   a.) Oxalic Acid

   b.) Copper Sulphate

   c.) Phenol

   d.) Iodoform

100. The color of stomach contents will turn Slate due to this poison:

   a.) Oxalic Acid

b.) Copper Sulphate

c.) Phenol

d.) Mercury

101. Administration by Oral gavage of a test compound that is highly metabolized by the liver vs subcutaneous injection will most likely result in:

   a.) More systemic toxicity

   b.) More local irritation at the site of administration caused by the compound

   c.) lower levels of metabolites in the systemic circulation

   d.) Less parent compound present in the systemic circulation

102. Which external sign indicates the phenol poisoning in Urine Sample?

   a.) Olive color

   b.) red color

   c.) Strong Odor of Urine

   d.) Yellow color

103. What method is used to isolate Chloral Hydrate poison?

   a.) Mineralization

   b.) Extraction method

   c.) Steam Distillation

   d.) Chromatographic method

104. The vessel for collection of the distillate of Cyanide poisoning by steam distillation method must contain:

   a.) Solution of Sodium Chloride

   b.) Solution of Sodium Hydroxide

   c.) Solution of Chloride Acid

   d.) Solution of Iodine

105. 'Black foot' disease is caused by _____

   a.) Chromium

   b.) Mercury

   c.) Arsenic

d.) Lead

106. A blackened Perforated nasal septum is an indication for addiction to:
    a.) Alcohol
    b.) Barbiturates
    c.) Hashish
    d.) Methamphetamine

107. Color that can be observed in nitric acid toxicity is
    a.) Yellow
    b.) Blue
    c.) Green
    d.) Red

108. Brown colored urine is seen in poisoning due to:
    a.) Carbon Monoxide
    b.) Nitric Acid
    c.) Sulphur
    d.) Arsenic

109. Cadmium is a highly toxic metal that causes:
    a.) Damage to renal tubules
    b.) GI tract irritation
    c.) Cancer
    d.) All

110. 'Itai-itai' disease is caused by_____
    a.) Cadmium
    b.) Mercury
    c.) Lead
    d.) Copper

111. What is the meaning of Itai Itai desease?
    a.) Painful
    b.) Ouch, Ouch

c.) Disease

d.) None

112. In Itai Itai disease which parts/Organ of body affected?

   a.) Kidney and bones

   b.) Heart and Lungs

   c.) Whole body

   d.) Hands and Legs

113. _____uses paralysis of respiratory muscles.

   a.) Barbiturates

   b.) Heroin

   c.) Botulinum

   d.) All of the above

114. A person with hot skin, dry mouth, talking irrelevant, dilated pupils, staggering gait and slurred speech. The most probable diagnosis is

   a.) Alcohol intoxication

   b.) Organophosphorous poisoning

   c.) Dhatura poisoning

   d.) Carbamates poisoning

115. A chemical substance that affects the processes of the mind or body and used in the diagnosis, treatment, or prevention of a disease:

   a.) Medicine

   b.) Barbiturates

   c.) Poison

   d.) Drug

116. Any type of natural or synthetic matter/substance which can cause grave harm or death or any psychological disturbance if inhaled, ingested or absorbed via skin, is known as:

   a.) Drug

   b.) Poison

   c.) P-DMAB

   d.) Beverages

Forensic Toxicology

117. Paraquat Poisoning causes:
    a.) Renal failure
    b.) Cardiac failure
    c.) Respiratory failure
    d.) Multiple organ failure

118. Cyanosis is caused by:
    a.) A Decreased concentration of Oxyhemoglobin
    b.) A Decreased concentration of Hemoglobin
    c.) An Increased concentration of reduced hemoglobin
    d.) An Increased concentration of Oxyhemoglobin

119. Which of the following toxicity can occur due to single exposure?
    a.) Acute toxicity
    b.) Sub-chronic toxicity
    c.) Chronic toxicity
    d.) Sub-acute toxicity

120. Ecstasy toxicity causes:
    a.) Hypereflexia
    b.) Trismus
    c.) Dilated pupils & Visual Hallucinations
    d.) All of the above

121. A person has bought a bottle of liquor from local shop and consumes it and within 1 hour of consumption he start vomiting, he develops blurred vision and confusions. He has been brought to the hospital in emergency situation. He should be treated with:
    a.) Diazepam
    b.) Barbiturates
    c.) Ethanol
    d.) Ethyl alcohol

122. All of the following are treatment options for toxic alcohol poisoning, except:
    a.) Fomepizole

b.) Hydroxycobalamin

c.) Thiamine

d.) Folic acid

123. Widmark's formula is used for estimation of:

    a.) Cyanides

    b.) Arsenic

    c.) Benzene

    d.) Blood Alcohol

124. McEwan's sign is seen in

    a.) Alcohol Intoxication

    b.) Arsenic Poisoning

    c.) Cyanide Poisoning

    d.) Lead Poisoning

125. Fatal dose of Methyl Alcohol is:

    a.) 10 ml

    b.) 20 ml

    c.) 60 to 120 ml

    d.) 15 to 25 ml

126. Hyperthermia in a patient of poisoning is a pointer to all, except:

    a.) Ecstasy

    b.) Selective serotonin reuptake inhibitor

    c.) Salicylates

    d.) Chlorpromazine

127. Bluish discoloration of neck of tooth due to

    a.) Alcohol

    b.) Arsenic

    c.) Cyanide

    d.) Nicotine

128. Which one of the following color test's reagent is made up of Selenous acid?

a.) Mecke's Test

b.) Marquis Test

c.) Von-Urk's Test

d.) Chen's Test

129. The phrase that best defines "Toxicodynamics" is the

a.) Dynamic nature of toxic effects among various species

b.) Dose range between desired biological effects and adverse health effects

c.) Linkage between Dose and Exposure

d.) Linkage between Response and Dose

130. Sodium fluoride is added as preservative in the following concentration for chemical analysis of blood and urine:

a.) 150 mg/10 ml

b.) 50 mg/10 ml

c.) 10 mg/10 ml

d.) 200 mg/10 ml

131. Preservative used for preservation of viscera in all cases of poisoning but not in the case of acid poisoning (except carbolic acid):

a.) Saturated solution of Sodium Chloride

b.) 10% Formalin

c.) Alcohol

d.) Acetone

132. Preservative used for preservation of viscera for Acid poisoning except Carbolic acid Poisoning:

a.) Saturated solution sodium chloride

b.) Rectified Spirit

c.) Alcohol

d.) 10% Formalin

133. Preservative used for preservation of viscera in case of Carbon Monoxide Poisoning:

a.) Saturated solution sodium chloride

b.) Rectified Spirit

c.) A layer of Paraffin (to prevent escape of gas)

d.) 10% Formalin

134. Following Gaseous Poison have different types of Odour, Except:

a.) Hydrogen sulphide

b.) Ammonia

c.) Phosphine

d.) Carbon monoxide

135. In _____ poisoning, the gas has greater affinity combines easily with haemoglobin and make them unable to carry oxygen to various tissues of the body.

a.) Arsenic

b.) Mercury

c.) Carbon-mono oxide

d.) Benzene

136. Carbon Monoxide is:

a.) Soluble in water

b.) Miscible with water

c.) Insoluble in water

d.) None

137. In Micro Diffusion Technique (Feld Stein) reduction of palladium chloride to grey or black is positive for:

a.) Carbon Monoxide

b.) Hydrogen Sulphide

c.) Phosphine

d.) Chlorine

138. What is the mode of action of carbon monoxide (CO)?

a.) It reduces the oxygen absorption by directly or indirectly damaging the alveoli.

b.) It destroys the red blood cells.

Forensic Toxicology

    c.) Combines with hemoglobin to reduce oxygen carrying capacity of RBCs.

    d.) It alters the structure of the hemoglobin.

139. Preservative used for preservation of blood in case of Poisoning;
    a.) Potassium Oxalate and Sodium fluoride
    b.) 50% Formalin
    c.) Alcohol
    d.) Rectified Spirit

140. CSF is required to be preserved in :
    a.) Alcohol Poisoning
    b.) Arsenic Poisoning
    c.) Carbon monoxide poisoning
    d.) Copper Poisoning

141. Preservative used in urine sample for chemical analysis is:
    a.) Formalin
    b.) EDTA
    c.) Alcohol
    d.) Thymol

142. Elapidaes are:
    a.) Vasculotoxic
    b.) Neurotoxic
    c.) Musculotoxic
    d.) Nontoxic

143. Magnan's symptoms are characteristic symptoms of following poisoning:
    a.) Alcohol
    b.) Charas
    c.) Cocaine
    d.) Ecstasy

144. This poison can lead to sex perversion?

- a.) Alcohol
- b.) Charas
- c.) Cocaine
- d.) Ecstasy

145. Common toxicity target of inorganic mercuric salts and organic mercury is:
- a.) Heart
- b.) Liver
- c.) Kidney
- d.) Lungs

146. Using Ferric Chloride test in salicylate toxicity turns urine to:
- a.) Pink color
- b.) Purple Color
- c.) Black color
- d.) Red Purple

147. Burning sensation after exposure to chilli pepper is an example of:
- a.) Sensitization
- b.) Dermatitis
- c.) Chemesthesis
- d.) Receptor Activation

148. Which of the following toxins comes from the castor beans?
- a.) Ricin
- b.) THC
- c.) Pesticides
- d.) Strychnine

149. Fatal dose of Castor bean is:
- a.) 2mg for a man weighing 60kg
- b.) 6mg for a man weighing 60kg
- c.) 60mg for a man weighing 60kg
- d.) 30mg for a man weighing 60kg

Forensic Toxicology

150. Ricin was first used in to kill:
     a.) Boris Korczak, 1981
     b.) James Dalton Bell, 1997
     c.) Georgi Markov, 1978
     d.) Shannon Richardson, 2013

151. Which part of the castor plant is poisonous?
     a.) Leaf
     b.) Root
     c.) Seeds
     d.) Overall Plant

152. Hunan hand syndrome is produced by following:
     a.) Chili Seed
     b.) Castor Seed
     c.) Croton Seed
     d.) Marking Nut

153. One vial of 10 ml Antivenom serum can neutralize:
     a.) 6 mg of Russell's viper venom
     b.) 6 mg of Cobra venom
     c.) 4.5 mg of common krait venom
     d.) 4.5 mg of saw scaled viper venom
     e.) All of the above

154. Following term is refers to the capsule of papaver somniferum after opium has been extracted from it:
     a.) Poppy Seeds
     b.) Opium Extracts
     c.) Post Ka Doda
     d.) Extracted Poppy

155. Derivatives of Opium is:
     a.) Morphine
     b.) Codeine

c.) Heroine

d.) All

156. After smoking of the opium the left out residue is known as:

    a.) Opium leftover

    b.) Opium extracts

    c.) Dross Opium

    d.) Deodrized Opium

157. Deodrized opium is prepared by treating opium with which of the following?

    a.) Chlorofrom

    b.) Methyl Alcohol

    c.) Petroleum Ether

    d.) Acetone

158. The source of most analgesics narcotic is:

    a.) White Oliver

    b.) Marijuana

    c.) Dahlia

    d.) Opium

159. Scientific name of Opium is:

    a.) Papaver Sominiferum

    b.) Cannabis Sativa

    c.) Papa Sominiferus

    d.) Marijuana

160. The range of Papaverine in Opium is:

    a.) 10-20%

    b.) 0-0.5%

    c.) 0.5-1.3%

    d.) 0.2-1%

161. Which of the following substance of opium is used in Cough Syrups?

    a.) Morphine

b.) Codeine

c.) Thebaine

d.) Papaverine

162. All Parts of Opium poppy is known as:

　a.) Poppy Straw

　b.) Poppin

　c.) Poppy

　d.) Cannabis

163. Wilson's disease is associated with the accumulation of following metal-

　a.) Thalium

　b.) Copper

　c.) Arsenic

　d.) Zinc

164. Restriction enzymes are used in one of these techniques:

　a.) Polymerization

　b.) Sequencing

　c.) Genotyping

　d.) RFLP

165. Which of the following is commonly known as ecstasy?

　a.) Methamphetamine

　b.) Amphetamine

　c.) methylenedioxymethamphetamine

　d.) 3,4-methylenedioxymethamphetamine (MDMA).

166. Electrophoresis is mainly used for:

　a.) Separates the molecules

　b.) For DNA Extraction

　c.) Differentiate the biological sample

　d.) Separate the Electric Current

167. In the case of heavy metal or arsenic compound poisoning the following antidote is used:

a.) Methyl blue

b.) Vitamin B12

c.) Unithiol

d.) Glucagon

168. Antidote for Copper Poisoning

   a.) Penicillamine

   b.) Dimercaprol

   c.) EDTA

   d.) a & b

169. Calcium EDTA is use as Antidote for following metal poisoning:

   a.) Mercury

   b.) Antimony

   c.) Arsenic

   d.) Lead

170. The best antidote to be given in cases of ethylene glycol toxicities is:

   a.) Ethanol

   b.) Fomepizole

   c.) Methanol

   d.) Aniline

171. Antidote for acetaminophen/Paracetomol

   a.) Sodium Nitrate

   b.) EDTA

   c.) Dimercaprol

   d.) N-acetylcysteine

172. Milk of Magnesia or soap solution can be used in poisoning due to:

   a.) Alkali

   b.) Acids

   c.) Metal

   d.) Alkaloids

173. Chemical name of Milk of magnesia is:
    a.) Magnesium Hydroxide
    b.) Magnesium oxide
    c.) Magnesium sulphate
    d.) Magnesium carbonate

174. Parlidoxime is used in the treatment of this poison:
    a.) Phosphorus
    b.) Pyrethrins
    c.) Parathion
    d.) Endrin

175. In alkali poisoning _____ can be used.
    a.) Milk
    b.) Luke Warm Water
    c.) Tinned Juice or Vinegar
    d.) Lime

176. What specific antidote is used for Cyanide Poisoning?
    a.) EDTA
    b.) Sodium Nitrate
    c.) Fuller's Earth
    d.) Penicillamine

177. At barium salt poisoning such specific chemical antidote is used:
    a.) Potassium iodide
    b.) Sodium chloride
    c.) Sodium sulphate
    d.) Sodium carbonate

178. What specific antidote is used for poisoning by iron?
    a.) Deferoxamine
    b.) Bemegride
    c.) Penicillamine

d.) Protamine sulphate

179. What specific antidote is used for Organophosphate Poisoning?

   a.) Deferoxamine

   b.) Bemegride

   c.) Penicillamine

   d.) Atropine

180. Ethanol is used as an antidote in methanol poisoning because

   a.) Ethanol competes for choline esterase enzyme

   b.) Ethanol competes for choline ADH enzyme

   c.) Ethanol by product is formic acid

   d.) Ethanol is cheap and easily available

181. Which of the following is not the metabolite of ethanol?

   a.) Methanol

   b.) Ethanol

   c.) Acetic Acid

   d.) Acetone

182. MAcEwen's sign is a manifestation of massive intake of:

   a.) Ethanol

   b.) Arsenic

   c.) Opium

   d.) Methyl Alcohol

183. One of the following symptom is an indication of severe ethanol intoxication:

   a.) Euphoria

   b.) Furious behavior

   c.) Muscular incoordination

   d.) All of the above

184. Blindness can be caused by the following:

   a.) Methanol

   b.) Ethyl Alcohol

c.) Arsenic

d.) Morphine

185. Following comment is true regarding methanol toxicity.

    a.) Methanol causes direct toxicity to optical nerves after absorption.

    b.) Methanol is less toxic than ethanol.

    c.) Aldehyde dehydrogenase converts methanol into formaldehyde which causes blindness.

    d.) Alcohol dehydrogenase and aldehyde dehydrogenase converts methanol into formic acid which causes blindness.

186. At the time of isolating Methanol in steam distillation method for volatile poisons, methanol is collected in:

    a) Empty Vessel

    b) Vessel with Sodium Hydroxide

    c) Vessel with Hydrochloric Acid

    d) Cooled Vessel

187. Magnesium Oxide

    a.) Neutralizes acids

    b.) Absorb Acids

    c.) Precipitate Acids

    d.) Make Acid

188. The reference dose (RfD) is generally determined by applying which of the following default procedures?

    a.) An uncertainty factor of 100 is applied to the NOAEL in chronic animal studies

    b.) a risk factor of 1000 is applied to the NOAEL in chronic animal studies

    c.) an uncertainty factor between 10,000 and 1 million is applied to the NOEL from chronic animal studies

    d.) a risk factor of 10,000 is applied to the NOAEL in subchronic animal studies

189. The most common target organ of toxicity is the:

    a.) Stomach

b.) Eyes

c.) Central Nervous System

d.) Lungs

190. Less affected Organs in human from toxicity:

a.) Muscle And Bone

b.) Hematopoietc system and lungs

c.) Brain And Peripheral Nerves

d.) Liver And Kidney

191. *"Ames Test"* is used to detect:

a.) Hepatotoxic potential of chemicals in cell cultures

b.) Salmonella typhimurium infection

c.) Mutagenic potential of chemicals using in vitro test with mutant strains of Salnonella typhimurium

d.) Solamonella typhi infection

192. Mineralization of the biological samples when heating in the crucible to high temperature at free air is named:

a.) Extraction

b.) Dry Ashing

c.) Distillation

d.) Wet Ashing

193. Which scientist was the first to suggest the idea of the necessity of the mineralization in the study of the biological material for the presence of heavy metal compounds:

a.) Ravdanikis P. K

b.) Krilova A. N.

c.) Nelyubin A. P

d.) Zaykovskiy F. V.

194. Which one of the following metallic poison is isolated from the biological matter with the help of mineralization destruction?

a.) Silver

b.) Thallium

c.) Cadmium

d.) Mercury

195. For the prevention of mercury loss during forensic-toxicological study of the biological material some special isolation method is used. This method is named:

a.) Destruction

b.) Disintegration

c.) Mineralization

d.) Denaturation

196. What method is used for isolation of mercury compounds from the biological material?

a.) Mineralization

b.) Destruction

c.) Steam distillation

d.) Extraction with acidified ethanol

197. A drug that induces Changes in perception and mood without affecting brain activity is known as:

a.) Stimulant

b.) Hallucinogen

c.) Dizziness

d.) Mood Swing

198. _____ is the process of removing nitric, nitrogenous, nitrososulphuric acids and nitrogen oxides from the mineralizate.

a.) Denitration

b.) Mineralization

c.) Denaturation

d.) Destruction

199. What method of the denitration is the most widespread and fast?

a.) Distillation

b.) By urea

c.) By formalin

d.) Hydrolysis

200. What reagent is used for denitration?

   a.) Sodium sulphite

   b.) Urea

   c.) Sodium of thiosulphate

   d.) Solution of formaldehyde

201. Which scientist suggested the method of the mineralizate denitration using formaldehyde?

   a.) Krylova A. N.

   b.) Zaykovskiy F. V.

   c.) Kramarenko V. F

   d.) Shvaykova M. D

202. Whit precipitate was obtained in the process of metallic poison isolation from the biological material. The mineralization was carried out by the mixture of H_2SO_4 and HNO_3. Following poison can be presence:

   a.) Lead

   b.) Thallium

   c.) Copper

   d.) Zinc

203. What metallic poison is detected with KI by the reaction of "gold rain formation"?

   a.) Cu^{2+}

   b.) Pb^{2+}

   c.) Ag^+

   d.) Ba^{2+}

204. Amenorrhoea and infertility are the possible complications of chronic poisoning with:

   a.) Mercury

   b.) Lead

   c.) Zinc

d.) Chromium

205. Ciguatera toxin is produced by:
    a.) Jelly Fish
    b.) Star Fish
    c.) Shark
    d.) Barracuda Fish

206. Malformation of Tooth Enamel is caused by:
    a.) Fluoride
    b.) CO
    c.) Iron
    d.) Lithium

207. When studying the mineralizate for the presence of barium cations the reaction with sodium rhodizonate is used which produce this color:
    a.) Black
    b.) Purple
    c.) Red
    d.) Yellow

208. _____ is also known as "Thorn Apple"?
    a.) Dhatura Stramonium
    b.) Hashish
    c.) Dhatura
    d.) Mushrooms

209. Ganja is Obtained From which part of Cannabis Plant:
    a.) Leaves
    b.) Twigs
    c.) Flowering Tops
    d.) Roots

210. Hashish is Produced from
    a.) Leaves of Cannabis Indica
    b.) Roots of Cannabis Indica

c.) Resin Exudate of Cannabis Indica

d.) Twigs of Cannabis Indica

211. _____ also used as an "Arrow Poison" :

a.) Nux Vomica

b.) Hashish

c.) Cocaine

d.) Arsenic

212. The cannabis plant secretes a sticky resin known as: :

a.) Nux Vomica

b.) Hashish

c.) Cocaine

d.) Arsenic

213. _____ known as Sweet Poison:

a.) Cyanide

b.) Aconite

c.) Phosphine

d.) Methanol

214. Which type of Phosphorus highly Toxic?

a.) Yellow Phosphorus

b.) Red Phosphorus

c.) Black Phosphorus

d.) Green Phosphorus

215. Yellow phosphorus oxidises with formation of pale yellow fumes glowing around after exposure to air. This phenomenon is known as:

a.) Glowing of phosphorus

b.) Phosphorus oxidation

c.) Phosphorescence

d.) Yellow glow

216. Which type of Phosphorus is Non-Toxic?

a.) Yellow Phosphorus

b.) Red Phosphorus

c.) Black Phosphorus

d.) Green Phosphorus

217. Which substance is used in sides of match box?

   a.) Yellow Phosphorus

   b.) Sulphur

   c.) Red Phosphorus

   d.) Potassium Chlorate

218. Phosphorus will spontaneously ignite if exposed to air in 30^0C, that's why it kept in following solution:

   a.) Formaldehyde

   b.) Water

   c.) Kerosene oil

   d.) b & c

219. When you strike and burn a match, it releases _____:

   a.) Carbon dioxide

   b.) Carbon monoxide

   c.) Methane

   d.) Sulphur dioxide

220. Surma (Collyrium for the eyes) is :

   a.) Tetra-ethyl Lead

   b.) Lead acetate

   c.) Lead Oxide

   d.) Lead Sulphide

221. Red Lead or Vermillion is:

   a.) Lead Acetate

   b.) Lead Carbonate

   c.) Lead Tetraoxide

   d.) Lead Oxide

222. Least Toxic Form of Lead is:

- a.) Tetra-ethyl Lead
- b.) Lead acetate
- c.) Lead Oxide
- d.) Lead Sulphide

223. Sideroblastic anemia is seen in poisoning with
    - a.) Mercury
    - b.) Lead
    - c.) Arsenic
    - d.) Cyanide

224. All are features of Lead Poisoning, except:
    - a.) Abdominal Pain
    - b.) Nephropathy
    - c.) Diarrhea
    - d.) Encephalopathy

225. Burton's line seen in Poisoning with?
    - a.) Yellow Phosphorus
    - b.) Lead
    - c.) Sulphur
    - d.) Potassium Chlorate

226. Average fatal period of Lead poisoning is :
    - a.) 2-4 hours
    - b.) 10-15 hours
    - c.) In few minutes
    - d.) 1-2 days

227. Toxicity of lead depends on which factor?
    - a.) Solubility
    - b.) Exposure
    - c.) Insolubility
    - d.) All of the above

Forensic Toxicology

228. _____ is the earliest sign of lead poisoning.
    a.) Concussion mercurialis
    b.) Eczema
    c.) Mees lines
    d.) Punctate Basophilia

229. Mercury is the only metal that is _____ in room temperature.
    a.) Solid
    b.) Liquid
    c.) Semi-Solid
    d.) Vapor

230. Fatal dose of Thallium:
    a.) About 1gm
    b.) About 1.5gm
    c.) About 2-3gm
    d.) About 4gm

231. Croton Tiglium is:
    a.) Arandi
    b.) Jamal gota
    c.) Gunchi
    d.) Chillies

232. The active principle of Croton Tiglium is:
    a.) Ricin
    b.) Abrin
    c.) Crotin
    d.) None

233. Arrange the following in the increasing order of their active principle:
    a.) Charas, Bhang, Hashish oil, ganja
    b.) Bhang, ganja, Charas, Hashish oil
    c.) Bhang, Hashish oil, Charas, ganja

Forensic Toxicology

    d.)   Charas, Hashish oil, ganja, Bhang

234. In case of drug abuse during pregnancy following specimens would be suitable:
   a.) Meconium
   b.) Hair
   c.) Urine
   d.) a & b

235. Adverse reaction to drugs prescribed by Doctor is known as:
   a.) Corrosive poisoning
   b.) Idiosyncrasy
   c.) Iatrogenic Poisoning
   d.) Poisoning

236. BAL full Form:
   a.) Bi-Anti Liquid
   b.) British Anti-Lewisite
   c.) British Anti-Liquid
   d.) British Acute-Liquid

237. BAL is a common name of :
   a.) Dimercaprol (2,3-dimercaptopropanol)
   b.) Dimercaprol (1,2-dimercaptopropanol)
   c.) Dimercaprol (1-dimercaptopropanol)
   d.) Diimercaprol (dimercaptopropanol)

238. BAL is effective against the effect of:
   a.) Phosphide poisoning
   b.) Heavy Metal Poisoning
   c.) Lead Poisoning
   d.) Arsenic Poisoning

239. BAL is antidote for the following metal poisons, but used to treat with EDTA for the following one:
   a.) Mercury

b.) Antimony

c.) Arsenic

d.) Lead

240. Which Vitamin is also a Hormone?

   a.) Vitamin C

   b.) Vitamin D

   c.) Vitamin B_{12}

   d.) Vitamin A

241. Poisoning From Carbolic Acid is known as:

   a.) Carbolic poisoning

   b.) Carbo Poison

   c.) Carbolism

   d.) Carbolic

242. In case of Carbolic Acid poisoning urine color turned olive green, this state is known as:

   a.) Carbolic poisoning

   b.) Carboluria

   c.) Carbolism

   d.) Carbolist

243. Which oil is used for stomach wash in carbolic acid poisoning?

   a.) Olive oil

   b.) Castor oil

   c.) Mustard oil

   d.) a & b

244. Phossy jaw is seen in which poisoning?

   a.) Red Phosphorus

   b.) Yellow Phosphorus

   c.) Arsenic

   d.) Carbamate

245. It is not Poisonous if taken by mouth:

a.) Arsenic

b.) Mercury

c.) Lead

d.) Thallium

246. Fatal dose of Mercuric Chloride:

a.) 0.5-1gm

b.) 1-2gm

c.) 5-10gm

d.) 2-3gm

247. Which of the following chelating agents is recommended for acute Lead Poisoning with signs of encephalopathy?

a.) Dimercaprol

b.) Calcium EDTA

c.) Dimercaprol+Calcium EDTA

d.) Succimer

248. All of the following symptoms can occur with Ciguatera poisoning, except:

a.) Metallic taste

b.) Flushing

c.) Myalgias

d.) Painful teeth

249. All of the following are treatment options for toxic alcohol poisoning, except:

a.) Fomepizole

b.) Thiamine

c.) Hydroxocobalamin

d.) Folic Acid

250. Ecotoxicology is the study of:

a.) Chemical Interaction of organism and environment

b.) Chemical Interaction of organism and animal

Forensic Toxicology

    c.) Physical Interaction of Organism and environment

    d.) Physical Interaction of organisms

251. Acute aquatic toxicity is measured in :

    a.) EC

    b.) ES

    c.) AC

    d.) AS

252. Which species is used as screening of chemicals:

    a.) Starfish

    b.) Zebrafish

    c.) Eisinia Foetida

    d.) Cat fish

253. Melamine can cause kidney stones by forming hydrogen bonds with:

    a.) Uric Acid

    b.) Cyanuric Acid

    c.) a & b

    d.) Nitric Acid

254. The interaction of melamine and cyanuric acid to cause renal toxicity is an example of:

    a.) Poisoning

    b.) Synergism

    c.) Antagonism

    d.) Potentization

255. Which category of insecticidal compounds presents a problem of persistent residues in fatty tissues of animals:

    a.) Organochlorines

    b.) Organophosphorus

    c.) Organophosphates

    d.) Carbamates

256. Which is not Anion?

a.) Halides

b.) Chlorate

c.) Nitrite

d.) Copper

257. Tear gas is also known as

a.) Chloroacetophenon

b.) Methylisocyanide

c.) Hydrogensulphide

d.) Chlorine

258. Which is not a Pesticide?

a.) Organophosphorous

b.) Organochloro

c.) Carbamates

d.) Sulphurdioxide

259. DDT full form is:

a.) Dichloro Diphenyl Trichloroethane

b.) Dichlorine Diphenolic Trichloro

c.) Di Diphenolic Trichloroethane

d.) Dichlo Diphenol Triethane

260. DDT is a:

a.) Organophosphorus Insecticides

b.) Organochloro Pesticides

c.) Carbamate Pesticides

d.) Organophosphrous Pesticides

261. What happens to DDT when it enters the body?

a.) It is water soluble and easily excreted out from the body.

b.) It is converted into an active metabolite.

c.) It bypasses the metabolism and excreted as such

d.) It is fat soluble and stored in fat tissue.

Forensic Toxicology

262. These are example of Synergism, except:
    a.) Alcohol & Barbiturates
    b.) Pyrethrins & Pyrethroid
    c.) Carbon Tetra Chloride & Ethanol
    d.) Codeine And Cannabis

263. Symptoms of Poisoning, except:
    a.) Vomiting
    b.) Diarrhoea
    c.) Coma
    d.) Chattering

264. Poisons commonly involved when symptom is Jaundice:
    a.) Carbon monoxide
    b.) Hepatotoxic
    c.) Arsenic
    d.) Cyanide

265. Hepatotoxic poisons are:
    a.) Arsenic
    b.) Carbon Tetrachloride
    c.) Vinyl Chloride
    d.) Flucoxacillin
    e.) All of the above

266. Human body shows symptom of Flushed Pink skin after being affected by these poisons, Except:
    a.) Alcohol
    b.) Cocaine
    c.) Cyanide
    d.) Carbon Monoxide

267. Red venous blood suggest poisoning from:
    a.) Cyanide
    b.) Alcohol

c.) Barbiturates

d.) Methaemoglobinaemia

268. Brown Arterial blood may suggest poisoning from:

a.) Cyanide

b.) Alcohol

c.) Barbiturates

d.) Methaemoglobinaemia

269. Urine may be cloudy or red or brown due to :

a.) Haematuria

b.) Haemoglobinuria

c.) Myoglobinuria

d.) All

270. Emetics are the Substance, which produce_____:

a.) Vomiting

b.) Sweating

c.) Diarrhea

d.) Pupil Dilation

271. Emesis should be avoided in_____:

a.) Corrosive Poisoning

b.) Ingestion of Petroleum distillates

c.) Coma

d.) All

272. Emetics are contraindicated in poisoning of:

a.) Arsenic

b.) Cyanide

c.) Kerosene

d.) Organophosphorus

273. Who are Arsenophagist?

a.) Who use Arsenic for laboratory purpose

Forensic Toxicology

    b.) Who use Arsenic in criminal activities

    c.) Who can tolerate Arsenic in high Doses

    d.) All of the above

274. Household emetics are:

    a.) Lukewarm water

    b.) Water with Salt

    c.) 15gm mustard powder in 200 ml of water

    d.) All of the Above

275. Method of emptying stomach of an unconscious patient is:

    a.) Luke warm water

    b.) Gastric Aspiration and Lavage

    c.) Zinc sulphate(1-2gm) in water(200ml)

    d.) Apomorphine

276. Demulcents should not be given in case of:

    a.) Phosphorus Poisoning

    b.) Strychinine Poisoning

    c.) Acid nitric

    d.) Alkalies

277. Bulky food like banana acts as a mechanical antidote for:

    a.) Arsenic

    b.) Barbiturates

    c.) Phosphorous

    d.) Glass

278. Strong concentrated alkalies are not used as antidote, because:

    a.) Production of big amount of CO_2

    b.) Production of toxic gases

    c.) Reducing the CO_2 amount

    d.) Decreasing the level of CO_2

279. Dilute Acetic Acid Neutralizes

a.) Acid

b.) Alkalis

c.) Phosphorus

d.) Lead

280. Acids Neutralizes by

   a.) Magnesium oxide or Calcium oxide

   b.) Lime

   c.) Copper sulphate

   d.) Tannin

281. Drug interact with their receptors sites by forming

   a.) Ionic bond

   b.) Hydrogen bond

   c.) Vander walls bond

   d.) All of the above

282. EDTA Full Form:

   a.) Ethylene Diamine Tetra Acetate

   b.) Ethyl Di Tetra Acetate

   c.) Ethylene Dioxy Tertiary Acetate

   d.) Ethyl Diamine Tetra Acid

283. Benzodiazepines are least effective in

   a.) Alcohol withdrawal syndrome

   b.) Obsessive-Compulsive Disorder

   c.) Phobias

   d.) All of the above

284. Benzodiazepines act on the CNS through the following mechanism:

   a.) Increasing the activity of GABA

   b.) Decreasing the activity of GABA

   c.) Pausing the activity of GABA

   d.) All of the above

285. Any material substance in the universe wherein the active constituents may be dispersed, accumulated, left, absorbed or chemically bound is known as:

   a.) Quantitation

   b.) Matrix

   c.) Toxic

   d.) None of above

286. Its involves separation of a crystalloid from a colloid by filtering through a semi-permeable membrane:

   a.) Dialysis

   b.) Sublimation

   c.) Partition

   d.) Absorption

287. _____ is applicable to isolate a toxicant in solid matrices.

   a.) Dialysis

   b.) Sublimation

   c.) Absorption

   d.) Partition

288. The extraction of metals in biological matrices may be carried out by the following methods:

   a.) Dry Ashing Method

   b.) Wet Digestion or Acid Digestion Method

   c.) Fresenius and Babo Method

   d.) All of the above

289. Opium poisoning is treated with:

   a.) Naloxone

   b.) Atropine

   c.) Neostigmine

   d.) Physostigmine

290. CAGA questionnaire is a widely used screening test for:

   a.) Alcohol Problem

- b.) Opium Poisoning
- c.) Barbiturate Poisoning
- d.) Heavy Metal Poisoning

291. Which method is suitable for mercury:
   - a.) Dry Ashing Method
   - b.) Fresenium and Babo Method
   - c.) Wet Digestion Method
   - d.) Selective Chemical Treatment

292. Erethism occours in:
   - a.) Mercury
   - b.) Lead
   - c.) Copper
   - d.) Arsenic

293. Lead encephalopathy is most commonly seen in:
   - a.) Pregnant woman
   - b.) Old person
   - c.) Children
   - d.) Painters

294. Which method is used to extract Toxic Anions from Forensic Matrices?
   - a.) Protein Precipitation
   - b.) Dialysis
   - c.) Micro diffusion
   - d.) All of the above

295. This method is useful for preliminary analysis of alkaloids, tranquilizing drugs and barbiturate etc.:
   - a.) Ammonium Sulphate Method
   - b.) Stas-otto method
   - c.) Selective Chemical Method
   - d.) Wet Digestion Method

Forensic Toxicology

296. Which Volatile Poison is not Miscible with Water?
   a.) Acetaldehyde
   b.) Acetone
   c.) Isopropyl Alcohol
   d.) Benzene

297. Which Volatile Poison is Slightly Soluble in Water?
   a.) Aniline
   b.) Carbon di-sulphide
   c.) Chloroform
   d.) Naphthalene

298. The substance used by athletes for doping is:
   a.) Marijuana
   b.) Barbituric Acid
   c.) Nandrolone
   d.) Lysergic Acid

299. A practice, in which poisons use to ingest to build immunity against toxic substance is known as:
   a.) Antibiotic
   b.) Mithridatism
   c.) Antitoxic
   d.) Tolerance

300. Which Volatile Poison has a Burning Taste?
   a.) Formaldehyde
   b.) Arsine
   c.) Ethyl Alcohol
   d.) Isopropyl Alcohol

301. Boiling range of Kerosene is:
   a.) 98-100°C
   b.) 150-300°C
   c.) 300-400°C

d.) 50-100°C

302. Domestic kerosene is blue, due to:
    a.) Anthracene
    b.) Coomassie Brilliant Blue
    c.) Anthraquinone
    d.) Eosine

303. Which volatile poison is oil?
    a.) Kerosene
    b.) Nitrobenzene
    c.) Turpentine
    d.) All of the above

304. A child aged about 11 year ingested a clear liquid, he vomited twice, had cough with tachypnea. After 24 hours bronchopneumonia also developed. These symptoms can be of following poisoning:
    a.) Ethanol
    b.) Methanol
    c.) Kerosene oil
    d.) Phenol

305. Characteristic Hexagonal crystals of iodoform are seen in Iodoform test indicates the presence of:
    a.) Acetone
    b.) Acetaldehyde
    c.) Pyridine
    d.) Carbondisulphide

306. Formation of Purple color in Schiff's reagent test confirms the presence of:
    a.) Acetone
    b.) Methanol
    c.) Formaldehyde
    d.) Ethyl Alcohol

Forensic Toxicology

307. Formation of deep blue in Sulphomolybdic Acid indicates the presence of:
    a.) Acetone
    b.) Acetaldehyde
    c.) Formaldehyde
    d.) Ethyl Alcohol

308. Schiff's reagent Test for Methanol produce:
    a.) Blue color
    b.) Pink Color
    c.) Purple color
    d.) Black Color

309. Violet color observed in Chromotropic Acid Test, this can be present:
    a.) Methanol
    b.) Ethanol
    c.) Ethyl Alcohol
    d.) Isopropyl Alcohol

310. Fujiwara Test is Preliminary Test For:
    a.) Arsenic
    b.) Mercury
    c.) Phosphorus
    d.) Chloroform

311. Fujiwara Test produces which color for confirmation of Chloroform?
    a.) Brown to black color
    b.) Pink to Red Color
    c.) Brown to Yellow Color
    d.) White Precipitate

312. The Scott Test is a Preliminary Colorimetric Method to analyze:
    a.) Heroin
    b.) Cocaine
    c.) Barbiturates

d.) Opium

313. Prussian Blue Test indicates the presence of:
   a.) Ethanol
   b.) Kerosene
   c.) Hydrocyanic Acid
   d.) Turpentine

314. Pink color observed in Cobalt Thio-Cyanate Test, Following Compound Present:
   a.) Heroin
   b.) Caffeine
   c.) Cocaine
   d.) Diazepam

315. Yellow crystals forms in Picric Acid test indicates the presence of:
   a.) Nicotine
   b.) Nitrobenzene
   c.) Hydrocyanic Acid
   d.) Naphthalene

316. Roussin's Test produced crystalline ruby red needle shape crystals indicates the presence of:
   a.) Nicotine
   b.) Naphthalene
   c.) Ethylene
   d.) Phenyl

317. Vitalis Test performed for detection of:
   a.) Dhatura
   b.) Arsenic
   c.) Morphine
   d.) Hashish

318. Alkaline beam Test performed for detection of:
   a.) Dhatura

Forensic Toxicology

    b.) Arsenic

    c.) Morphine

    d.) Hashish

319. Odor of rotten eggs is a characteristic odor of which gaseous poison?

    a.) Carbon Monoxide

    b.) Hydrogen Sulphide

    c.) Ammonia

    d.) Sulphur dioxide

320. Odor of decaying fish is a characteristic odor of which gaseous poison?

    a.) Carbon Monoxide

    b.) Hydrogen Sulphide

    c.) Phosphine

    d.) Sulphur dioxide

321. Odor of Shoe Polish is a characteristic odor of which poison?

    a.) Nitrobenzene

    b.) Hydrogen Sulphide

    c.) Ammonia

    d.) Sulphur dioxide

322. Odor of Coal Gas is characteristic odor of which poison?

    a.) Malathion

    b.) Hydrogen Sulphide

    c.) Ammonia

    d.) Sulphur dioxide

323. Odor of Garlic is characteristic odor of these poisons, Except:

    a.) Malathion

    b.) Arsenic

    c.) Sulphur dioxide

    d.) Parathion

324. Which one of the following poison smell like Freshly Mown Hey?

a.) Sulfur Di-Oxide

b.) Phosgene

c.) Isopropanol

d.) Lewisite

325. When Hydrochloric Acid combined with certain oxidizing chemicals, it can turns into following toxic gas that may cause harm to the skin, eyes and respiratory system:

a.) Carbon Monoxide

b.) Chlorine

c.) Hydrogen Sulphide

d.) Phosphine

326. Which one of the following is use into a wide variety of plastic products, lubricating oils, nail polish, hair spray, etc., and their consumption may cause serious health issues?

a.) Propane

b.) Ethane

c.) Phthalates

d.) Chlorine

327. Which gaseous poison converts Methemoglobin to Sulphametemoglobin?

a.) Carbon Monoxide

b.) Hydrogen Sulphide

c.) Phosphine

d.) Chlorine

328. Prussian blue is Anti-dote for:

a.) Mercury

b.) Thalliium

c.) Arsenic

d.) Lead

329. Calcium Gluconate or edenate is Anti-dote for:

a.) Mercury

b.) Antimony

c.) Magnesium Sulfate

d.) Lead

330. Vomited matter is blue or green turns to deep blue on adding ammonia solution in poisoning from:

a.) Copper

b.) Antimony

c.) Arsenic

d.) Lead

331. In Reinsch Test Purple-Black color is observed which indicates the presence of:

a.) Arsenic

b.) Antimony

c.) Mercury

d.) Thallium

332. Apple Green Flame observed in Flame test which indicates the presence of:

a.) Arsenic

b.) Antimony

c.) Barium

d.) Thallium

333. A Shiny Black deposit on the Copper strip in Reinsch Test indicates the presence of:

a.) Bismuth

b.) Antimony

c.) Mercury

d.) Thallium

334. If Turmeric Paper Strip turns red; following poison is present:

a.) Arsenic

b.) Cadmium

c.) Boric Acid

d.) Acetic Acid

335. In test with Hydrogen Sulphide Yellow precipitate indicates the presence of:
   a.) Arsenic
   b.) Cadmium
   c.) Mercury
   d.) Thallium

336. A bright pink spot surrounded by blue circle produced in Test with Dinitro-P-Diphenyl Carbazide indicates the presence of:
   a.) Arsenic
   b.) Cadmium
   c.) Mercury
   d.) Thallium

337. In Chemical tests for Chromium following color produced:
   a.) Red
   b.) Yellow
   c.) Black
   d.) Brown

338. In Iron poisoning, bloody vomiting and diarrhea, massive fluid loss in GIT, renal failure and death occur in:
   a.) Stage I
   b.) Stage II
   c.) Stage III
   d.) Stage IV

339. Shining Silvery deposit on copper are observed in Reinsch Test indicates the presence of:
   a.) Arsenic
   b.) Mercury
   c.) Chromium
   d.) Manganese

Forensic Toxicology

340. A green color observed in urotropine test, following compound is present:
    a.) Strychnine
    b.) Brucine
    c.) Opium Alkaloids
    d.) Cannabis Sativa

341. Test with Lead Acetate produce Golden yellow plates which indicates the presence of:
    a.) Flavonoid
    b.) Barium
    c.) Chromium
    d.) Arsenic

342. Nitrogen-Phosphorus Detector (NPD) is used to detect_____:
    a.) Pesticides
    b.) Volatile poison
    c.) Gaseous poison
    d.) Metals

343. The dried LSD in long wavelength UV will produced:
    a.) Red Color
    b.) Blue Fluorescence
    c.) Purple Color
    d.) Yellow

344. Extract + Marquis develop violet color which indicates the presence of:
    a.) Morphine
    b.) Codein
    c.) Charas
    d.) Heroin

345. Extract + Conc. Nitric Acid (HNO_3) develop bright Orange Yellow color which indicates the presence of:
    a.) Morphine

b.) Codeine

c.) Charas

d.) Heroin

346. Extract + Mandelin's develop Dark Reddish Brown color which indicates the presence of:

a.) Morphine

b.) Codeine

c.) Charas

d.) Heroin

347. Extract + Marquis develop Reddish Purple color which indicates the presence of:

a.) Morphine

b.) Codeine

c.) Charas

d.) Heroin

348. Extract + Conc. Nitric Acid (HNO_3) develop Pale Yellow color which indicates the presence of:

a.) Morphine

b.) Codeine

c.) Charas

d.) Heroin

349. Extract + Mandelin's develop Reddish Brown color which indicates the presence of:

a.) Morphine

b.) Codeine

c.) Charas

d.) Heroin

350. Extract + Marquis develop Dark Violet color which indicates the presence of:

a.) Morphine

b.) Codeine

c.) Charas

d.) Heroin

351. Extract + Conc. Nitric Acid (HNO_3) develop Greenish Yellow color which indicates the presence of:

a.) Morphine

b.) Codeine

c.) Charas

d.) Heroin

352. Extract + Mandelin's develop Olive Green color which indicates the presence of:

a.) Morphine

b.) Codeine

c.) Charas

d.) Heroin

353. Extract + Marquis Reagent develop Yellow/Orange color which indicates the presence of:

a.) Benzodiazepines

b.) Alkaloids

c.) Methaqualone

d.) Phenothiazines

354. Extract + FPN Reagent develop Orange red/violet red/Blue color which indicates the presence of:

a.) Benzodiazepines

b.) Alkaloids

c.) Methaqualone

d.) Phenothiazines

355. In McNally's Test a red color formed if _____ is present.

a.) Salicylic Acid

b.) Barbiturates

c.) Phenol

d.) Aspirin

356. Salicylic acid as a medication is used in following disease-
    a.) Mental illness
    b.) Cancer
    c.) Skin disease
    d.) All of the above

357. Keshan disease is a condition caused by deficiency of the following mineral:
    a.) Selenium
    b.) Polonium
    c.) Thallium
    d.) Barium

358. Neurotic Plant Poison is:
    a.) Strychnos Nux Vomica
    b.) Papaver Somniferum
    c.) Nicotiana Tabacum
    d.) Ergot

359. Spinal Plant Poison is:
    a.) Strychnos Nux Vomica
    b.) Papaver Somniferum
    c.) Nicotiana Tabacum
    d.) Taxus baccata

360. Cerebral Plant Poison is:
    a.) Strychnos Nux Vomica
    b.) Papaver Somniferum
    c.) Nicotiana Tabacum
    d.) Cannabis Indica

361. Cardiac Plant Poison is:
    a.) Strychnos Nux Vomica
    b.) Papaver Somniferum
    c.) Nicotiana Tabacum

Forensic Toxicology

    d.) Cannabis Sativa

362. Irritant Plant Poison is:
   - a.) Strychnos Nux Vomica
   - b.) Abrus Precatorius
   - c.) Nicotiana Tabacum
   - d.) Cannabis Sativa

363. What's the name of the poison found in deadly nightshades, which is also used in eye surgery?
   - a.) Atropin
   - b.) Ricin
   - c.) Capsaicin
   - d.) Scopolamine

364. What is a common treatment in case of ingestion of the toxic oleander plant?
   - a.) Antibiotics
   - b.) Vomiting
   - c.) Stomach Pumping
   - d.) Bulky foods

365. Fatal period of Cannabis Sativa:
   - a.) 1-2 hours
   - b.) 3-4 hours
   - c.) 5 hours
   - d.) Hours to days

366. Fatal period of Narium Odorum also known as White Oleander (Kaner):
   - a.) 5-15 min
   - b.) 1-2 hours
   - c.) 24-36 hours
   - d.) 4-5 hours

367. Dile-Koppanyi test for Barbiturates gives color:

a.) Red

b.) Black

c.) Purple

d.) Yellow

368. Which one of the following pairs of drug and indication is accurate:

   a.) Amhetamine:Alzheimer's dementia

   b.) Bupropion:Acute anxiety

   c.) Fluxetine:Insomania

   d.) Ropinirole:Parkinson's Disease

369. Which of the following dermatologic findings and potential causes is incorrect?

   a.) Cyanosis – Methemoglobinemia

   b.) Erythroderma – Boric Acid

   c.) Pallor – Carbon Monoxide

   d.) Jaundice – Hypercarotinemia (excess carrot intake)

370. Both hepatic and renal toxicity can be caused by :

   a.) CCl_4

   b.) Arsenic

   c.) Copper sulphate

   d.) All of the above

371. In treatment of corrosive poisoning, which of the following is not used?

   a.) Antacids

   b.) Intravenous Fluid

   c.) Bulky food

   d.) Gastric Lavage

372. Gastric Lavage is contraindicated in poisoning with:

   a.) Organophosphorus Compounds

   b.) Arsenic

   c.) Barbiturates

d.) Sulphuric Acid

373. Sulphuric acid is:
   a.) Hygroscopic
   b.) Hydroscopic
   c.) Both a & b
   d.) None of the above

374. Lethal dose of Camphor for adult is:
   a.) 4-6 gm
   b.) 2 gm
   c.) 1 gm
   d.) 0.4gm

375. Which of the following poison retard putrefaction?
   a.) Organophosphorus
   b.) Carbolic Acid
   c.) Oxalic Acid
   d.) Hydrochloric Acid

376. Glass blowers shakes are seen in poisoning due to:
   a.) Arsenic
   b.) Mercury
   c.) Lead
   d.) Copper

377. Mercury affect this part of Kidney:
   a.) PCT
   b.) Loop of Henle
   c.) DCT
   d.) Collection duct

378. Average Fatal Period of Copper Poisoning:
   a.) 4 hrs
   b.) 24-48 hours

c.) 18-36 hours

d.) Hours to Days

379. Toxic Substance commonly used by washer men to put marks on clothes:

   a.) Croton tiglium

   b.) Semecarpusanacardium

   c.) Plumbagorosea

   d.) Calotopisprocera.

380. Which of the following snake is poisonous:

   a.) Krait

   b.) Cobra

   c.) Black Mamba

   d.) All of the above

381. Cobra poison is :

   a.) Myotoxic

   b.) Neurotoxic

   c.) Cardiotoxic

   d.) Hemotoxic

382. Krait poison is :

   a.) Myotoxic

   b.) Neurotoxic

   c.) Cardiotoxic

   d.) Hemotoxic

383. Viper snake poison is :

   a.) Myotoxic

   b.) Neurotoxic

   c.) Cardiotoxic

   d.) Hemotoxic

384. Venom of sea snake is mostly

   a.) Myotoxic

- b.) Neurotoxic
- c.) Cardiotoxic
- d.) Hemotoxic

385. A toxalbumin similar to viperine snake venom is present in the seeds of:
    - a.) Dhatura
    - b.) Abrus Precatorius
    - c.) Ergot
    - d.) Cannabis

386. The study of Poisoning of Human and Animals by plant is known as:
    - a.) Plant Toxicology
    - b.) Toxicology
    - c.) Forensic Plantology
    - d.) Phytotoxicology

387. Ophotoxemia refers to:
    - a.) Organophosphorous poisoning
    - b.) Scorpion venom poisoning
    - c.) Snake venom poisoning
    - d.) Heavy metal poisoning

388. The most useful bedside test to suggest snake bite envenomation is:
    - a.) Platelet count
    - b.) 20 min whole blood clotting time
    - c.) Prothrombin time
    - d.) International normalized ratio

389. The use of antitoxin in the treatment of snakebite is an example of:
    - a.) Synergism
    - b.) Medical Treatment
    - c.) Chemical Antagonism
    - d.) Functional Antagonism

390. Which of the following snake is non-poisoning snake?

Forensic Toxicology

    a.) Viper

    b.) Krait

    c.) Cobra

    d.) Rat snake

391. Which pain relieving drug should be avoided in snake bite poisoning?

    a.) Tramadol

    b.) Morphine

    c.) Aspirin

    d.) Paracetamol

392. Narcotic drugs are categorized as:

    a.) Antibiotics

    b.) Anti-inflammatory

    c.) Analgesics

    d.) Poisonous Substance

393. When a drug user adheres to the regular schedule of drug intake then he develops:

    a.) Withdrawal Sickness

    b.) Abstinence Syndrome

    c.) Mental Sickness

    d.) Physical Dependency

394. Which of the following is not a side effect of Digoxin?

    a.) Bradycardia

    b.) Yellow vision changes

    c.) Scooping of the T segment on ECG

    d.) Hypokalemia

395. Substances, which reduce arousal and stimulation is known as:

    a.) Depressants

    b.) Barbiturates

    c.) Hallucinogens

    d.) Narcotic Drugs

Forensic Toxicology

396. Heroin is made by reacting morphine with:
    a.) Ethyl Alcohol
    b.) Methyl Alcohol
    c.) Acetic Acid
    d.) Acetic Anhydride

397. Which is considered as synthetic opiates?
    a.) Morphine
    b.) Codeine
    c.) Heroine
    d.) Methadone

398. All are characteristic features of Acute Morphine Poisoning, Except:
    a.) Pinpoint Pupil
    b.) Low Blood Pressure
    c.) Slow labored Breathing
    d.) Hyperpyrexia

399. Ganja is obtained from which part of the cannabis plant?
    a.) Resin
    b.) Flower Top
    c.) Leaf
    d.) Fruits

400. A potent form of Marijuana is known as:
    a.) Coca derivatives
    b.) THC
    c.) Sinsemilla
    d.) Hashish

401. The active components of cannabis responsible for its hallucinogenic properties are the:
    a.) Cannabinols
    b.) TetrahydroCannabis (THCs)
    c.) Tetrahydrocannabinols (THCs).

d.) Tetrahallucinogeniccannabinols (THCs)

402. THCs is:
    a.) An Alkaline
    b.) Acidic Substance
    c.) A fat soluble oleoresin
    d.) Derivative

403. Which form of cannabis has the highest concentration of THCs?
    a.) Heroin
    b.) Cannabis Oil
    c.) Methadone
    d.) Hashish

404. Which one of the following drug of abuse is over 100 to 300 times more potent than morphine?
    a.) Fentanyl
    b.) Psilocybe
    c.) Mescaline
    d.) Mandrex

405. Ethylene Glycol in Antifreeze, first Affects:
    a.) Brain
    b.) Kidney
    c.) Liver
    d.) Central Nervous System

406. The Duquenois-levine test is a color test for:
    a.) Barbiturates
    b.) Marijuana
    c.) Acidic Poison
    d.) Alcohol

407. Growing substance to suggest that nicotine has its effects by:
    a.) Releasing Serotonin into the Cerebellum
    b.) Releasing GABA into the hypothalamus

Forensic Toxicology

    c.)   Releasing Dopamine in mesolimbic system of the brain

    d.)   Releasing Acetykholine into the Diencephalons

408. LSD Full form:
    a.) Lysergic Acid Diethylamide
    b.) Lysergic Alkali Diethylamide
    c.) Lysergic Strychnine Diethylamide
    d.) Lysergic Acid Disulphide

409. The effect if LSD was first described by
    a.) Adolf Bare
    b.) Albert Holfmann
    c.) Aristotle
    d.) Charak

410. Mixture of PCP(Phencyclidine) and Lysergic Acid Diethylamide is known as:
    a.) Narcotic Drug
    b.) Weed
    c.) Angel Dust
    d.) Crack

411. Crack is a term used for:
    a.) Marijuana
    b.) Barbituric Acid
    c.) Amphetamine
    d.) Cocaine

412. Speedballs is a combination of heroin and?
    a.) Cocaine
    b.) Codeine
    c.) Thebaine
    d.) Papaverine

413. Barbiturates are the derivatives of :
    a.) Marijuana

- b.) Barbituric Acid
- c.) Lysergic Acid
- d.) Alcohol

414. Barbiturates was first synthesized by:
    - a.) Adolf Von Baeyer
    - b.) Albert Hofmann
    - c.) Aristotle
    - d.) Charak

415. Which one is a long acting barbiturate?
    - a.) Barbital
    - b.) Phenobarbital
    - c.) Pentobarbital
    - d.) Amobarbital

416. In which poisoning color of urine appears Liquid Gold?
    - a.) Arsenic
    - b.) Mercury
    - c.) Barbiturates
    - d.) Phosphorus

417. Which color test turns orange brown in the presence of amphetamines?
    - a.) Marquis Test
    - b.) Scott Test
    - c.) Gutzeit Test
    - d.) Play of Colors

418. Cocaine is extracted from:
    - a.) Cannabis Sativa
    - b.) Opium
    - c.) Poppy straw
    - d.) Erythroxylum coca

419. Cocaine is extracted from which part of Erythroxylum coca?

a.) Stems

b.) Roots

c.) Dried Leaves

d.) Fruits

420. Visual and tactile hallucination with black staining on tongue and teeth is because of:

a.) Heroin

b.) Cannabis Oil

c.) Cocaine

d.) Hashish

421. Feelings of sands under skin or moving insects on skin which cause itching, because of:

a.) Alcohol withdrawal

b.) Morphine Poisoning

c.) Organophosphorus poisoning

d.) Cocaine Poisoning

422. Megnan's Syndrome is seen in case of:

a.) Heroin poisoning

b.) Cocaine Poisoning

c.) Mercury Poisoning

d.) Alcohol Poisoning

423. The most reliable method for estimating blood alcohol level is:

a.) Cavett's Method

b.) Breath analyzer

c.) Thin Layer Chromatography

d.) Gas Liquid Chromatography

424. Which type of poisoning is responsible for Oxalate crystal in urine?

a.) Mercury Poisoning

b.) Arsenic Poisoning

c.) Ethylene Glycol Poisoning

d.) Cocaine Poisoning

425. What specific antidote is used for Ethylene Glycol Poisoning?
   a.) Deferoxamine
   b.) Bemegride
   c.) Penicillamine
   d.) Fomepizole

426. Insecticides are a class of:
   a.) Volatile Poisons
   b.) Non Volatile Poisons
   c.) Organic Poisons
   d.) Organic Non Volatile Poisons

427. Organophosphorus insecticides are considered as derivatives of:
   a.) Phosphonic Acid
   b.) Phosphoric Acid
   c.) Corresponding Acids
   d.) a & b

428. Which of the following is used as a chromogenic spray agent in TLC of Organophosphorus insecticides?
   a.) Cobalt acetate-o-toulidine Reagent
   b.) Mercurous Nitrate Reagent
   c.) Potassium Iodate- starch Reagent
   d.) All of the above

429. SLUDGE are symptoms produced by:
   a.) Organophosphorus compounds
   b.) Carbamates
   c.) Organochloro Compound
   d.) Barbiturates

430. Stripping is a process used for:
   a.) Separation
   b.) Absorption

c.) Purification

d.) Cleaning

431. The best specimen for drug and poison screening is:

   a.) Blood

   b.) Hair

   c.) Urine

   d.) Nails

432. Sensor Based gas analyzer is used for the extraction of:

   a.) Non Volatile Poison

   b.) Gaseous Poison

   c.) Volatile Organic Poison

   d.) Pesticides

433. Electro dialysis digestion is the extraction method for:

   a.) Non Volatile Inorganic Poison

   b.) Gaseous Poison

   c.) Volatile Organic Poison

   d.) Pesticides

434. Nestler's Reagent test is Applied for:

   a.) Mercury

   b.) Chloral Hydrate

   c.) Ammonia

   d.) Carbon Monoxide

435. Assertion (A): The volatile compounds can be analyzed by GLC.

   Reason (R): Because volatile compounds gets precipitated with inert gas in the column.

   a.) Both (A) and (R) are correct

   b.) Both (A) and (R) are correct but (R) is not the correct explanation of (A)

   c.) (A) is False but (R) is True

   d.) (A) is True but (R) is False

436. Assertion (A): Ethyl Alcohol forms Metabolite formaldehyde in the body.

Reason (R): Because Formaldehyde is the metabolic end product of Ethyl Alcohol in the body.

a.) Both (A) and (R) are correct

b.) Both (A) and (R) are correct but (R) is not the correct explanation of (A)

c.) (A) is False but (R) is True

d.) (A) is True but (R) is False

437. Match the Scientist With his Findings and Research:

Scientist	Findings
a.) MJB Orfila	(i) Father of Nerve Agents
b.) Gerhard Schrader	(ii) Father of Forensic Toxicology
c.) Paul Hermann Muller	(iii) Author of 'Silent Spring'
d.) Rachel Carson	(iv) Synthesized DDT

Code:

	(a)	(b)	(c)	(d)
a.)	(i)	(ii)	(iii)	(iv)
b.)	(ii)	(i)	(iv)	(iii)
c.)	(iv)	(iii)	(ii)	(i)
d.)	(iii)	(ii)	(i)	(iv)

438. Match the Following:

List-I Poisons	List-II Actions
a.) Phenol	(i) Deliriant
b.) Dhatura	(ii) Cardiac
c.) Calatropis	(iii) Irritant
d.) Aconite	(iv) Corrosive

Code:

	(a)	(b)	(c)	(d)
a.)	(ii)	(iii)	(iv)	(i)
b.)	(iv)	(i)	(iii)	(ii)
c.)	(iii)	(ii)	(i)	(iv)
d.)	(i)	(iv)	(ii)	(iii)

439. Match the Following Cannabis plant parts on the basis of percentage of THC content find in them.

    List-I
    Parts
    a.) Pistillate flower
    b.) Leaves
    c.) Stalks
    d.) Roots

    List-II
    THC %
    (i) 1-2%
    (ii) 10-12%
    (iii) 0.1-0.3%
    (iv) <0.03%

    Code:

	(a)	(b)	(c)	(d)
a.)	(vi)	(i)	(ii)	(iii)
b.)	(iii)	(ii)	(i)	(iv)
c.)	(ii)	(i)	(iii)	(iv)
d.)	(i)	(iv)	(ii)	(iii)

440. Disulfiram is used for treatment of chronic alcohol abuse acts by:
    a.) Increasing the concentration of acetaldehyde
    b.) Blocking aldehyde dehydrogenase
    c.) Blocking acetate dehydrogenase
    d.) a & c

441. Soxhlet extractor was invented by:
    a.) Karl Landsteiner
    b.) Amboise Pare
    c.) Franz Von Soxhlet
    d.) Paracelsus

Forensic Toxicology

442. In the analysis of Poisons, the sequence of events in chronological order is

   a.) Group tests, Extraction, Tissue Homogenisation and specific tests.

   b.) Extraction, Group tests, Tissue Homogenisation and specific tests.

   c.) Tissue Homogenisation, Extraction, Group tests, and specific tests.

   d.) Extraction, Tissue Homogenisation, Group tests and specific tests.

443. A 35 year old female was found burnt in the kitchen. An empty can of kerosene with little quantity at bottom was found nearby. Match box and few sticks were found on the parapet. She has sustained 100% burns. Black soot was present on the body. Smell of kerosene was observed. Pugilistic attitude was present. Burns from superficial to deep were present on the body. Soot particle were present in trachea. Carboxyhaemoglobin of 15% concentration was reported on analysis. No evidence of mechanical injuries was observed on the body. The room was bolted from the inside. The cause of death was:

   a.) Carbon Monoxide Poisoning

   b.) Postmortem Burns

   c.) Asphyxia due to soot

   d.) Antemortem burns

444. Chloral hydrate comes under the following category:

   a.) Tranquilizer

   b.) Hypnotic

   c.) Hallucinogen

   d.) Analgesic

445. Quantitative estimation of ethyl alcohol can be done properly in:

   a.) Urine

   b.) Blood

   c.) Saliva

   d.) a & b

446. Ethanol is produced by the fermentation of sugar by:

   a.) Yeast

   b.) Glycerine

c.) Yoghurt

d.) Alkaloid

447. Which is false?

a.) At pH 7.4 Salicylic Acid is in the unionized form.

b.) When alkalinizing the urine, serum K+ replacement may be required.

c.) Hemodialysis is of benefit.

d.) A serum salicylate level of 2.0 at 6 hours is sufficient for medical discharge.

448. Which of the following term is used to describe the dose of a drug required to kill 50% population under study:

a.) ED99

b.) ED50

c.) LD50

d.) LD1

449. What is the full form of LD50?

a.) Lethal Dose 50

b.) Legal Death 50

c.) Lysergic Dose 50

d.) Least Dose 50

450. Which is true about the LD50?

a.) Dose of a substance to which 50% of Population do not show any response.

b.) Dose of a substance which kills 50% of Population exposed.

c.) 50% of the dose of a substance which can kill an Population.

d.) 50 mg/kg dose of a substance to test the toxic responses in Population.

451. Organic mercury targets_____ whereas inorganic mercury primarily targets_____.

a.) Bones, ligaments

b.) Nervous system, kidneys

c.) Hematopoietic system, nervous system

d.) Liver, nervous system

452. 1 ppm is equivalent to:
 a.) 1 g/kg
 b.) 1 µg/kg
 c.) 1 mg/kg
 d.) 1 mg/100g

453. Which Scientist suggested the use of Palatal rugae for identity verification:
 a.) Harrison Allen
 b.) Ambroise Pare
 c.) Arstotle
 d.) 1 mg/100g

454. Which is the wrong mechanism of action for the listed drug/toxin?
 a.) Colchicine: binds to intracellular tubulin preventing cell mitosis
 b.) Amanita phalloides: impairs DNA synthesis
 c.) Strychnine: inhibits glycine in the spinal cord
 d.) Isoniazid: reduces folate activity

455. Which of the following is use in Molotov cocktail?
 a.) Gasoline
 b.) Magnesium
 c.) Arsenic
 d.) Mercury

456. Which of the following is not an Insecticide?
 a.) Fluoroacetamide
 b.) Malachite green
 c.) Nicotine
 d.) Malathion

457. Which Liquid poison is considered a dangerous chemical due to its extremely foul odor? This is also known as smelliest chemical.

Forensic Toxicology

- a.) Cadaverine
- b.) Butyric acid
- c.) Thioacetone
- d.) Ethyl Mercaptan

458. Thioacetone is dangerous because:
    - a.) It is explosive
    - b.) It is flammable
    - c.) It has worst smell
    - d.) All of the above

459. These are Blood agents, Except:
    - a.) Hydrogen Cyanide
    - b.) Arsine
    - c.) Cyanogen
    - d.) Sarin

460. This blood agent also act as a choking agent:
    - a.) Hydrogen Cyanide
    - b.) Phosgene
    - c.) Arsine
    - d.) Cyanogen

461. This blood agent also act as a Blister agent:
    - a.) Hydrogen Cyanide
    - b.) Phosgene
    - c.) Vinyl Arsine
    - d.) Cyanogen

462. Each of the following statement is true about Oxalic Acid, Except:
    - a.) It is Corrosive
    - b.) It may contribute to kidney stones
    - c.) Large exposures may lead to pulmonary edema
    - d.) Ingestion of soluble oxalates is not harmful

463. Which statement is false?
    a.) VX is odorless and tasteless.
    b.) Production of Thioacetone led to the evacuation of the German city of Freiburg in 1889.
    c.) Very short contact with fumes or small quantities of the liquid of Hydrogen Fluoride can cause severe, painful burns.
    d.) There is no Antidote for Nerve Agents.

464. Which of the following toxins is not produced by bacteria?
    a.) Cholera toxin
    b.) Aflatoxin
    c.) Botulinum toxin
    d.) Diphtheria toxin

465. Ergotism is associated with toxin produced by _____:
    a.) Plant
    b.) Fungus
    c.) Virus
    d.) Mycoplasma

466. Aspergillus species produce Aflatoxins, Aflatoxin B1. One of the aflatoxins causes following toxic effects in humans:
    a.) Severe liver toxicity and Carcinogenesis
    b.) It is less toxic due to its natural origin
    c.) Cardiotoxicity
    d.) Respiratory collapse

467. Tetrodotoxin, a deadly toxin, is found in _____:
    a.) Rattle snake
    b.) Mussels
    c.) Puffer fish
    d.) Scorpion

468. Which is the most likely toxic effect of cosmetics?
    a.) Skin corrosion

b.) Allergic contact dermatitis

c.) Local muscular degeneration

d.) Major risk of systemic toxicity after absorption of

469. Gastrointestinal tract does not have any profound effect on nature of ingested chemicals:

   a.) True

   b.) False

   c.) Gut-microflora plays important role in biotransformation of ingested chemicals

   d.) It does not matter whether gastrointestinal tract have any effects on chemicals

470. Which of the following is the main way of transportation of a lipid soluble toxicant within body?

   a.) Filtration

   b.) Endocytosis

   c.) a & b

   d.) Passive diffusion

471. What is the most common toxicity target of ethanol (beverage alcohol) in humans?

   a.) Fetus

   b.) Liver

   c.) Kidneys

   d.) Heart

472. What are the common targets of ethanol toxicity in humans?

   a.) Liver, brain, heart and kidneys

   b.) Liver, lungs and intestine

   c.) Liver, brain and fetus

   d.) Spleen, liver, brain and thymus

473. Which part of the body is primarily affected by caffeine intoxication?

   a.) Heart

   b.) Brain

c.) Liver

d.) Kidneys

474. Leaves from the following plants are the significant source of caffeine.

   a.) Coffea arabica

   b.) Erythroxylum coca

   c.) Cola acuminata

   d.) Camellia sinensis

475. Exposure to _____ is associated with occupation.

   a.) Aflatoxins

   b.) Formaldehyde

   c.) Ethanol

   d.) Acetaminophen

476. Exposure to _____ is associated with lifestyle.

   a.) Chromium

   b.) Benzidine

   c.) Nicotine

   d.) Asbestos

477. Which statements is true regarding GHB (gamma hydroxybutyrate)?

   a.) Is a psychoactive drug of abuse

   b.) It has been used clinically to treat narcolepsy, as an anesthetic agent, to treat alcohol withdrawal and in body building.

   c.) It has a very short elimination half-life (30 mins) and thus may not be detectable in a urine sample taken after delay of several hours.

   d.) All of the above

478. _____ is a most widely used Rodenticides and Pesticides.

   a.) Brodifacoum

   b.) Tetradotoxin

   c.) Batrachotoxin

   d.) All of the above

479. Which statement is false about Lithium toxicity?

Forensic Toxicology

a.) Toxicity associated with chronic use occurs at lower serum levels

b.) In a non-user an acute overdose may not be symptomatic until the serum level is greater than 3

c.) Most effects of acute OD are neurological

d.) Appropriate management of an acute OD could include charcoal, IV fluids and haemodialysis

480. Repeated High exposure of _____ to the body can lead to bone disease.

    a.) Chromium

    b.) Benzidine

    c.) Nicotine

    d.) Sodium Fluoride

481. With regard to snake bite which is true?

    a.) There is no specific sea snake antivenom.

    b.) Tiger and brown snakes are more less likely to cause paralysis than black snake.

    c.) The dose of antivenom needed for tiger snake envenomation is usually one vial.

    d.) The antivenom should be diluted 1in 10 in normal saline and given over half an hour.

482. Comparing the Red-Back and the Funnel Web Spiders, which is false?

    a.) Female Red-back and Male Funnel Web are harmful.

    b.) Death due to the bite from Funnel Web Spider can happen within 15min-1hour.

    c.) The Red-Back Spider venom is rabbit based and given with little risk of allergy.

    d.) Severe toxicity with Red-Back Spider envenomation takes at least three hours.

483. Kim Jong-Nam (half-brother of Kim Jong-Un, who is currently leader of North Korea) was killed by spray of this poison:

    a.) Trimethylamine Oxide

    b.) Hydrogn Selenide

c.) VX

d.) None of the above

484. Trimethylamine oxide is found in_____:

a.) Marine Fish

b.) Snakes

c.) Bacteria

d.) All of the above

485. What does Hydrogen Selenide Smell like?

a.) Rotten fish

b.) Mustard seeds

c.) Rotten eggs mixed with rotten radishes

d.) Feces

486. Mesothelioma (cancer of lining covering internal organs) is associated with exposure to _____:

a.) Nickel

b.) Mercury

c.) Benzene

d.) Asbestos

487. Asbestos made from?

a.) From naturally occurring fibrous minerals.

b.) From Bacteria.

c.) From Fish.

d.) From Artificial.

488. All statements are true about symptoms of Sulfur Mustard, except:

a.) Sulfur mustard sometimes smells like garlic, onions or mustard and sometimes it has no odor.

b.) Sulfur mustard is naturally in the environment.

c.) Mild respiratory distress to marked airway damage.

d.) Exposure to sulfur mustard usually is not fatal.

489. Which gas was leaked in Bhopal gas Tragedy in 1984?

a.) Carbon monoxide

b.) Hydrocyanic acid

c.) Methyl Isocyanate

d.) Styrene Gas

490. Which gas was leaked in Vizag (Visakhapatnam) gas Tragedy in 2020?

a.) Carbon monoxide

b.) Hydrocyanic acid

c.) Methyl Isocyanate

d.) Styrene Gas

491. One of the following method is best to avoid aspiration of fluids during gastric lavage in a comatose patient:

a.) Introduction of a cuffed endotracheal tube before lavage

b.) Keeping the head of the patient at a lower level than his feet

c.) Putting the patient in the left lateral position

d.) Continuous suction of the fluid from the trachea

492. Heneicosane is a characteristic component of which of the following?

a.) Kerosene

b.) Petrol

c.) Diesel

d.) Oils

493. Pristane and phytane are present only in which of the following?

a.) Heavy Petroleum Distillate

b.) Medium Petroleum Distillate

c.) Light Petroleum Distillate

d.) Gasoline

494. Gastric lavage turned black when it was healed after being treated with silver nitrate, this can be seen in following poisoning:

a.) Parathion

b.) Malathion

c.) Celphos

d.) Arsenic

495. Sui/Sitari are prepared from:
 a.) Croton Tiglium
 b.) Cannabis sativa
 c.) Abrus Precatorius
 d.) Morphine

496. Priapism occurs in:
 a.) Cantharides
 b.) Phosphorus
 c.) Mercury
 d.) a & b

497. "Ewing's postulate" refers to:
 a.) Relationship between Trauma and Tumor
 b.) Complications result from trauma
 c.) The role of disease in modifying the effects of trauma
 d.) Congenital abnormalities caused by drugs

498. Reed's classification is use for:
 a.) Grade of dead body
 b.) Grade of toxicity
 c.) Grade of loss of consciousness
 d.) Grade of loss of blood

499. Prolonged Prothrombin time occurs in cases of poisoning with:
 a.) Thallium
 b.) Thioacetone
 c.) Warfarin
 d.) Hydrocyanic acid

500. New born is more sensitive to following toxicity than an adult:
 a.) DDT
 b.) Lead

c.) Malathion
d.) b & c

Answer-Sheet

Forensic Toxicology

1	b	2	c	3	d	4	a	5	b	6	d	7	a	8	a	9	d	10	b
11	c	12	b	13	a	14	a	15	c	16	d	17	c	18	d	19	c	20	a
21	d	22	c	23	d	24	a	25	d	26	b	27	f	28	b	29	e	30	b
31	b	32	d	33	d	34	d	35	c	36	c	37	c	38	e	39	d	40	c
41	b	42	d	43	b	44	b	45	a	46	d	47	b	48	a	49	a	50	d
51	c	52	c	53	a	54	b	55	c	56	a	57	c	58	a	59	b	60	d
61	d	62	b	63	a	64	b	65	a	66	d	67	b	68	a	69	d	70	c
71	c	72	a	73	c	74	c	75	a	76	c	77	c	78	a	79	c	80	b
81	a	82	d	83	c	84	a	85	d	86	b	87	a	88	c	89	b	90	d
91	c	92	a	93	d	94	c	95	a	96	c	97	a	98	c	99	b	100	d
101	d	102	a	103	c	104	b	105	c	106	d	107	a	108	b	109	d	110	a
111	b	112	a	113	c	114	c	115	d	116	b	117	d	118	c	119	a	120	d
121	d	122	b	123	d	124	a	125	c	126	d	127	d	128	a	129	d	130	b
131	a	132	b	133	c	134	d	135	c	136	c	137	a	138	c	139	a	140	a
141	d	142	b	143	c	144	c	145	c	146	b	147	c	148	a	149	b	150	c
151	d	152	a	153	e	154	c	155	d	156	c	157	c	158	d	159	a	160	c
161	b	162	a	163	b	164	d	165	d	166	a	167	c	168	d	169	d	170	b
171	d	172	b	173	a	174	c	175	c	176	b	177	c	178	a	179	d	180	b
181	d	182	a	183	c	184	a	185	d	186	d	187	a	188	a	189	c	190	a
191	c	192	b	193	c	194	d	195	a	196	b	197	b	198	a	199	c	200	d
201	b	202	a	203	b	204	b	205	d	206	a	207	c	208	a	209	c	210	c
211	a	212	b	213	b	214	a	215	c	216	b	217	c	218	b	219	d	220	d
221	c	222	d	223	b	224	c	225	b	226	d	227	a	228	d	229	b	230	a
231	b	232	c	233	b	234	d	235	c	236	b	237	a	238	b	239	d	240	b
241	c	242	b	243	d	244	b	245	b	246	b	247	c	248	b	249	c	250	a
251	a	252	b	253	c	254	b	255	a	256	d	257	a	258	d	259	a	260	b
261	d	262	d	263	d	264	b	265	e	266	b	267	a	268	d	269	d	270	a

Forensic Toxicology

271	d	272	c	273	c	274	d	275	b	276	a	277	d	278	a	279	b	280	a
281	d	282	a	283	b	284	a	285	b	286	a	287	b	288	d	289	a	290	a
291	b	292	a	293	c	294	d	295	a	296	d	297	c	298	c	299	b	300	c
301	b	302	c	303	d	304	c	305	b	306	c	307	d	308	c	309	a	310	d
311	b	312	b	313	c	314	b	315	d	316	a	317	a	318	d	319	b	320	c
321	a	322	d	323	c	324	d	325	b	326	c	327	b	328	b	329	c	330	a
331	b	332	c	333	a	334	c	335	b	336	b	337	a	338	a	339	b	340	c
341	a	342	a	343	b	344	a	345	a	346	a	347	d	348	d	349	d	350	b
351	b	352	b	353	a	354	d	355	a	356	c	357	a	358	b	359	a	360	d
361	c	362	b	363	a	364	c	365	d	366	c	367	c	368	d	369	c	370	d
371	d	372	d	373	a	374	a	375	b	376	b	377	a	378	c	379	b	380	d
381	b	382	b	383	d	384	a	385	b	386	d	387	c	388	b	389	c	390	d
391	c	392	c	393	d	394	d	395	a	396	d	397	d	398	d	399	b	400	d
401	c	402	c	403	b	404	a	405	d	406	b	407	c	408	a	409	b	410	c
411	d	412	a	413	b	414	a	415	b	416	c	417	a	418	d	419	c	420	c
421	d	422	b	423	d	424	c	425	d	426	d	427	d	428	d	429	a	430	c
431	c	432	b	433	a	434	c	435	b	436	b	437	b	438	b	439	c	440	d
441	c	442	c	443	a	444	b	445	d	446	a	447	d	448	c	449	a	450	b
451	b	452	c	453	a	454	d	455	a	456	b	457	c	458	c	459	d	460	b
461	c	462	d	463	d	464	b	465	b	466	a	467	c	468	b	469	c	470	d
471	b	472	c	473	b	474	d	475	b	476	c	477	d	478	a	479	d	480	d
481	d	482	c	483	c	484	a	485	c	486	d	487	a	488	b	489	c	490	d
491	a	492	c	493	a	494	c	495	c	496	d	497	a	498	c	499	c	500	d

Notes

BIBLIOGRAPHY AND SUGGESTED READING

- Some questions have been taken from different competitive examinations question papers.

- The Merck Veterinary Manual (2016). Chapter "Herbicide Poisoning" by PK GUPTA 11th edition, Merck & Co. Inc Whitehouse Station, NJ, USA 2969-99

- *Textbook of Forensic Medicine and Toxicology, V. V. Pillay, 14th edition, p369.*

- Gupta PK (2016) Essential Concepts in Toxicology. Published by PharmaMed Press (A unit of BSP Books Pvt. Ltd), Hyderabad, India pp 362

- Anderson, M. E., R. S. Thomas, K. W. Gaido, et al. Dose - response modeling in reproductive toxicology in the systems biology era. *Reprod. Toxicol.* 19 : 327 – 337, 2005.

- Deighton, N. Metabolomics. In *Molecular and Biochemical Toxicology,* eds. R. C. Smart and E. Hodgson, pp. 67 – 79. Hoboken, NJ: Wiley, 2008.

- Edwards, S. W. and R. J. Preston. Systems biology and mode of action based risk assessment .*Toxically. Sci.* 106: 312 – 318, 2008.

- Harrill, A. H., P. K. Ross, D. M. Gatti, et al. Population - based discovery of toxicogenomics biomarkers for hepatotoxicity using a laboratory strain diversity panel. *Toxicol.Sci.* 110: 235 – 243, 2009.

- Merrick, B. A. Proteomics. In *Molecular and Biochemical Toxicology,* eds. R. C. Smart and E. Hodgson, pp. 41 – 66. Hoboken, NJ: Wiley, 2008.

- National Research Council. Toxicity testing in the 21st century: A vision and a strategy.

- Washington, DC: National Research Council Committee on Toxicity Testing and Assessment of Environmental Agents, National Academy Press, 2007.

- Olelsiak, M. F. Toxicogenomics. In *Molecular and Biochemical Toxicology,* eds. R. C. Smart and E. Hodgson, pp. 25 – 39. Hoboken, NJ: Wiley, 2008.

- Plant, N. Can systems toxicology identify common biomarkers of non - genotoxic carcinogenesis? *Toxicology* 254: 164 – 169, 2008.

- Smart, R. C. and E. Hodgson, eds. *Molecular and Biochemical Toxicology.* Hoboken, NJ: John Wiley and Sons, 2008.

- Stone, E. A. and D. M. Nielsen. Bioinformatics. In *Molecular and Biochemical Toxicology,* eds.

- R. C. Smart and E. Hodgson, pp. 81 – 107. Hoboken, NJ: Wiley, 2008.

- Waring, J. F., R. Ciurlionis, R. A. Jolly, et al. Microarray analysis of hepatotoxins in vitro reveals a correlation between gene expression profile les and mechanisms of toxicity. *Toxicol.Lett.* 120: 359 – 368, 2001.

- Joy, R. M. Neurotoxicology: Central and peripheral. In *Encyclopedia of Toxicology*, vol. 2, P. Wexler, ed. New York: Academic Press, 1998, pp. 389–413.

- Stryer, L. *Biochemistry*, 4th ed. San Francisco: W. H. Freeman, 1999.

- Eaton, D. L., and C. D. Klaassen. Principles of toxicology In *Casarrett and Doull's Toxicology: The Basic Science of Poisons*, 6th ed. C. D. Klaassen, ed. New York: McGraw-Hill, 2001, pp.11–34.

- Calabrese, E. J., and L. A. Baldwin. U-shaped dose-responses in biology, toxicology, and publichealth. *An. Rev. Public Health* 22: 15–33, 2001.

- Bondar, V. S. Toxicological chemistry. Schemes and Tables: Handbook for students of higher schools / V. S. Bondar, S. A. Karpushina. – Kharkiv: NUPh: Golden Pages, 2009. – 120 p.

- Karpushina, S. A. Toxicological chemistry. Lecture course / S. A. Karpushina, V. S. Bondar, I. A. Zhuravel. – Kharkiv: NUPh: Golden pages, 2011. – 208 p.

- Toxicological Chemistry. Laboratory workbook / S. A. Karpushina, I. A. Zhuravel, V. S. Bondar, S. V. Bayurka. – Kharkiv: NUPh, 2012. – 63 p.

- Baselt, C. R. Disposition of Toxic Drugs and Chemicals in Man: 9-th edition / R. C. Baselt. – California: Biomedical Publications, 2011. – 1900 p.

- Basic Analytical Toxicology / R. J. Flanagan [et al.]. – Geneva: World Health organization, 1995. – 363 p.

- Bell, S. Forensic Chemistry / S. Bell. – New Jersey: Pearson Prentice Hall. – 671 p.

- Clarke's analysis of drugs and poisons in pharmaceuticals, body fluids and postmortem material: 4-th edition / A. C. Moffat [et al.]. – London; Chicago: Pharmaceutical Press, 2011. – 2736 p.

- Clarke's Analytical Forensic Toxicology / ed. by Sue Jickells, Adam Negrusz. – London: Pharmaceutical Press, 2008. – 648 p.

- Flanagan, R. J. Developing Analytical Toxicology Services: Principles and Guidance [Electronic resource] / R. J. Flanagan. – Geneva: World Health Organization, 2005. – 36 p. – Available at: http://www.who.int/ipcs/publications/training_poisons/hospitalnalytical_toxicology.pdf (date of the application: (07.09.2017). – Developing Analytical Toxicology Services: Principles and Guidance.

- Gracia RC, Snodgrass WR. Lead toxicity and chelation therapy. Am J Health Syst Pharm. 2007 Jan 1; 64(1):45-53.

- Mann KV, Travers JD. Succimer, an oral lead chelator. Clin Pharm. 1991 Dec; 10(12):914-22.

- Patrick L. Lead toxicity, a review of the literature. Part 1: Exposure, evaluation, and treatment. Altern Med Rev. 2006 Mar; 11(1):2-22.

- Poisoning & Drug Overdose. Fourth Edition / ed. by Kent R. Olson. – Zange Medical Books, Mc Graw-Hill, 2004. – 718 p.

- https://en.wikipedia.org/wiki/History_of_poison.

- Kaviraja Ambikadutta Shastri: Editor, Susrutsamhita of Maharsi-Susruta Edited with AyurvedaTatva-Sandipika, Kalpasthana; Sthavarvish-vidnyaniyam Adhyaya: Chapter 2, Verse 33, Chaukhmba Sanskrit Sansthan Publication, Varanasi, Second Edition, part 1, 2010; 32 [45]

- Udayvir Shastri: Editor, Kautilaya Arthashasrta of Vishnugupta Kautalya Edited with 'Nayachandrika' Hindi Commentry, Volume 2, Ashumrutak Parikshan,Chapter no. 82, Verse 21-30.Bharat Bharti publication, Delhi, Second Edition.1969:135-137.

- https://en.wikipedia.org/wiki/History_of_poison.

- Dr. Parikh C.K., Parikh's Textbook of Medical Jourisprudence Forensic Medicine and Toxicology, Section VIII, Introduction to Toxicology, CBS Publishers & Distributors, Dehli, Sixth Edition Reprint-2007; 8(9).

- Dr. Mathiharan K, Dr. Patnaik AK.Modi's Medical Jurisprudence and Toxicology, Section 2,Diagnosis of Poisoning:Chapter 1,Lexis Nexis Publication, Dehli,Twenty Third Edition, 2006: 21-29

- Dr. U. R. Shekhar Namburi, editor. Agadtantra, Diagnosis of Poisoning, Chapter 05, 1st edition, Chaukhambha Sanskrit Sansthan Varanasi, 2013; 41 & 42.

- Dr. Brahmanand Tripathi, Editor, Charakasamhita of Agnivesha Edited with 'Charak-Chandrika' Hindi Commentary, Volume 2, Chikitsasthana; Vishachikitsaadhyaya, Chapter 23, verse 16, Chaukhmba Surbharati Prakashan, Delhi, Reprint, 2002; 749.

- Kaviraja Ambikadutta Shastri: Editor, Susrutsamhita of Maharsi-Susruta Edited with AyurvedaTatva-Sandipika, Kalpasthana; Sthavarvish-vidnyaniyam Adhyaya: Chapter 1, Verse 42, Chaukhmba Sanskrit Sansthan Publication, Varanasi, Second Edition, part 1, 2010; 08.

- Prof. K. R. Srikant Murthy, editor Ashtanga Sangraha of Vagbhata, Sutrasthana, Annaraksha Vidhi Adhyaya, 8/48, 9th edition, Chaukhmbha Orientalia, Varanasi, 2005; 167.

- Kaviraja Ambikadutta Shastri: Editor, Susrutsamhita of Maharsi-Susruta Edited with AyurvedaTatva-Sandipika, Kalpasthana; Sthavarvish-vidnyaniyam Adhyaya: Chapter 1, Verse 56, Chaukhmba Sanskrit Sansthan Publication, Varanasi, Second Edition, part 1, 2010; 11.

- Dr. Brahmanand Tripathi: Editor, Ashtanghrudayam of Shrimadvagbhata Edited with 'Nirmala Hindi commentary', Uttarasthan; Vishpratishedhadhyay, Chapter 35, Verse, 50-53, Chaukhmba Sanskrit Pratishthan, Delhi: Reprint, 2007; 1150.

- Udayvir Shastri: Editor, Kautilaya Arthashasrta of Vishnugupta Kautalya Edited with 'Nayachandrika' Hindi Commentry, Volume 2, Ashumrutak Parikshan, Chapter no. 82. Bharat Bharti publication, Delhi, Second Edition, 1969; 135-137.

- Dr. Parikh C.K., Parikh's Textbook of Medical Jourisprudence Forensic Medicine and Toxicology, Section 10, Fuels, 52, CBS Publishers & Distributors, Dehli, Sixth Edition Reprint-2007; 10.39.

- Bardale Rajesh, Principles of Forensic Medicine and Toxicology, Section 2, Toxicology:General Considerations:Chapter 33,The Health Science Publishers,Dehli,,Second Editon, 2017; 473-474.

- Dr. Parikh C.K., Parikh's Textbook of Medical Jourisprudence Forensic Medicine and Toxicology,Section VIII, Introduction to Toxicology, CBS Publishers & Distributors, Dehli, Sixth Edition Reprint-2007; 8.11.

- AK Jaiswal, Handbook of Forensic Analytical Toxicology, chapter no.4, Thin Layer Chromatography and its application, 1st edition, Jaypee publication Dehli, 2014; 139.

- http://plato.mercyhurst.edu/chemistry/kjircitano/ChemPrincLaboratories/Drugs.

- AK Jaiswal, Handbook of Forensic Analytical Toxicology, chapter no.5, Thin Layer Chromatography and its application, 1st edition, Jaypee publication Dehli, 2014; 214.

- Dr. Mathiharan K, Dr. Patnaik AK.Modi's Medical Jurisprudence and Toxicology, Section 2, Poisons and their Medicolegal Aspects: Chapter 1,Lexis Nexis Publication, Dehli,Twenty Third Edition, 2006; 29.

- https://www.eolss.net/Sample-Chapters/C09/E6-12-23-00.pdf.

- Blanke RV, Poklis A, Analytic/Forensic Toxicology In: Amdur MO, Doull J, Klaassen CD editors. Cascarett and Doull's Toxicology The Basic Science of Poisons.4th ed. London: Pergamon Press, 1992; 905-923.

- 54. Dr. Mathiharan K, Dr. Patnaik AK., Modi's Medical Jurisprudence and Toxicology, Section 2, Poisons and their Medicolegal Aspects: Chapter 1,Lexis Nexis Publication, Dehli, Twenty Third Edition, 2006; 29.

- http://plato.mercyhurst.edu/chemistry/kjircitano/ChemPrincLaboratories/Drugs.

- AK Jaiswal, Handbook of Forensic Analytical Toxicology, chapter no.12, Breath Alcohol Analyser and its application, 1st edition, Jaypee publication Dehli, 2014; 442-444.

- Broughton, P. M. G. A rapid ultraviolet spectrophotometric method for the detection, estimation and identification of barbiturates in biological material.
- *Biochem. J.* 63 (1956) 207.
- Clarke, E. G. C. (Ed.) *Isolation and Identification 0/ Drugs*(1969) Pharmaceutical Press, London, £14.00.
- Curry. A. S. *Simple Tests to Detect Poisoning. (1966)* Association of Clinical Pathologists Broadsheet No. 52,25p.
- Curry, A. S. *Poison Detection in Human Organs.* 2nd ed.(1969) Thomas, Springfield, £5.78.
- Dauphinais, R. M., McComb, R. A specific procedure for serum glutethimide (Doriden) determination. *Amer.J. C/in. Path.* 44 (1965) 440.
- Forrest, I. S., Forrest, F. M., Mason, A. S. A rapid urine colour test for imipramine (Tofranil, Geigy): supplementary report with colour chart. *Amer. J. Psychiat.* 116 (1960) 1021.
- Forrest, I. S., Forrest, F. M. Urine colour test for the detection of phenothiazine compounds. *C/in. Chem.* 6 (1960) 11.
- Garvey, K., Bowden, C. M. The colorimetric determination of barbiturates. *Proc. Assoc. din. Biochem.* 4 (1966) 20.
- Lawson, A. A. H., Brown, S. S. Acute methaqualone (Mandrax) poisoning. *Scot. med. J-.* 12 (1967) 63.
- Matthew, H., Lawson, A. A. H. *Treatment 0/ Common Acute Poisonings.* 2nd ed. (1970), Livingstone, Edinburgh,£1.00.
- Routh, J. I., Shane, N. A., Arredondo, E. G., Paul, W. D. Determination of N-acetyl-p-aminophtnol in plasma. *C/in. Chem.* 14 (1968) 882.
- Sunshine, I. *Handbook 0/ Analytical Toxicology. (1969)* Chemical Rubber Co., Cleveland, £14'00.
- Sunshine, I., Gerber, S. R. *Spectrophotometric Analysis 0/ Drugs.* Including Atlas of Spectra (1963) Thomas, Springfield, £4.50.
- Todd, R. G. (Ed.) *Extra Pharmacopoeia: Martindale,* 25th ed. (1967) Pharmaceutical Press, London, £7.50.
- Trinder, P. Rapid determination of salicylate in biological fluids. *Biochem. J.* 57 (1954) 301.
- Whitehead, T. P., Worthington, S. The determination of carboxyhaemoglobin. *C/in. chim. Acta* 6 (1961) 356.
- Kanji S, MacLean RD. Cardiac glycoside toxicity: more than 200 years and counting. Crit Care Clin. 2012 Oct; 28(4):527-35.

- Smith TW. Digitalis. Mechanisms of action and clinical use. N Engl J Med. 1988 Feb 11; 318(6):358-65.

- Wright RO et al. Methemoglobinemia: etiology, pharmacology, and clinical management. Ann Emerg Med. 1999 Nov;34(5):646-56.

- Schillinger BM et al. Boric Acid Poisoning. J Am Acad Dermatol. 1982 Nov;7(5):667-73.

- Piantadosi CA. Carbon monoxide poisoning. N Engl J Med. 2002 Oct 3;347(14):1054-5.

- Mazzone A, Dal Canton A. Image in clinical medicine. Hypercarotenemia. N Engl J Med. 2002 Mar 14;346(11):821.

- Hochholzer W. The facts behind niacin. Ther Adv Cardiovasc Dis. 2011 Oct;5(5):227-40.

MCQs on Forensic Medicine and Toxicology

www.ingramcontent.com/pod-product-compliance
Lightning Source LLC
Chambersburg PA
CBHW052348220526
45465CB00003BA/1012